KINGDOM of LIGHT /
kingdom of Darkness

Truth about Spiritual Warfare

KINGDOM of LIGHT I
kingdom of Darkness

Truth about Spiritual Warfare

by Michael R. Hicks

Christian Literature & Artwork
A BOLD TRUTH Publication

KINGDOM of LIGHT kingdom of Darkness
Copyright © 2015 by Michael R. Hicks
ISBN 13: 978-0-9965908-6-0

Printed in the United States of America

Bold Truth Publishing
606 W. 41st, Ste 4
Sand Springs, Oklahoma 74063
www.BoldTruthPublishing.com

The views expressed in this book are not necessarily those of the publisher.

Table of Contents

Foreword

As the years go by, we as a people are floating *away* from God. From Kings and Palaces to Prime Minister's offices and the White House, we as a people are falling away from THE TRUTH OF GOD. We as a people are *straying* from the concepts that God has laid out for us to be successful in life. We, as a people are adopting *lifestyles, ideas,* and *realities* that cause nations to *fall,* when other empires have fallen in the past from the exact same practices. And as we continue to *compromise* against the Word of God and the teachings of Christ Jesus; we too will fall.

This book is not meant to bash any people, religion or lifestyle but to simply tell THE TRUTH according to the Word of God. Many people have been *snared* by the *tricks, skits* and *shenanigans* of Satan and have *grown comfortable* in his *"live free"* from the ideals, nature and doctrine of the Kingdom of Light – his *anti*-God doctrine. This freedom will *cost us* our lives and most importantly, will cost us eternal life.

The True and Living God is a good God and He wants us to be successful in our lives upon the earth, but when we *run away* from home, *away from* the doctrine of life, we become *aliens* to the His Kingdom.

My prayer is to find our way back to God.

Michael Ray Hicks

Acknowledgments

I would like to dedicate this book
to the following people for their support:

Sonja Hicks,
Wilmer and Queen Hicks,
Doctor Mark A. Hick,
Mitch Mullen,
Brother Vince,
Duane Baker,
Jerome and Jackie Gates,
Jack Hawkins,
Mr. and Mrs. Paschal Thompson,
Open Skies Ministry,
Billy Joe and Sharon Daugherty,
Kenneth Hagin Sr.,
James Slim Crabtree,
John and Melissa Barrett,
Common Ground,
Promise Keepers,
Rhema Ministries,
Willie James and Pamela Hankerson,
Michael and Renee Norton,
Leoddis Clay,

Don Bowers,
Brian Wideman,
Tony Mac,
Gary and Sally Wisenbach,
Steve Young,
Dr. Coyette Morgan,
The Fire Ladies,
Brother Daryl Holloman,
Mike and Carol Moody,
Dove Christian Fellowship,
Robert McGown,
Truckers for Christ,
Alonzo and Marvinette Ponder,
Glenda Bishop,
Ron Qualls,
Bill Boyd,
Bob Jones,
The Full Gospel Believers
and The Body of Jesus Christ
Community Church

Prayer

Most gracious Heavenly Father
I thank You and I give You praise –
for You are God and God alone
I thank You for Your Grace and mercy that held me
Through the years
I thank You for Your salvation that changed my life forever
I thank You for the work that You have given me to do
I thank You for the ones who will read this book
And get an understanding of the spiritual warfare
That everyone is involved in
And I pray that we all get revelation knowledge
On who we are in Christ
And revelation knowledge that we are
In Christ Jesus
That we are the head and not the tail
That greater are You that lives in us than
the devil that is in the world
Speak to our hearts and reveal Yourself to us all
In Jesus name,
Amen

Chapter 1

What Happened?

First things first, God is good and Satan is bad devil. Do not ever get the two confused. There are millions of people that blame God for all types of disasters, acts of nature and so on. God is blamed for tornados, tsunamis, earthquakes, and a number of natural catastrophes, tragedies, and cataclysms. But most fail to realize that Satan is the prince of this world and all he wants to do is to steal, kill and destroy.

Just about every person on the planet is familiar with the story of Adam and Eve in the Garden of Eden. Just about every person knows that God gave Adam dominion over this planet. Just about every person knows that God made Adam the steward over His creation. Just about every person knows that God allowed him to name the animals and to tend His garden *(Genesis 1:26-28)*. Just about every person knows that God and Adam fellowshipped in the cool of the day. Just about every person knows that in the beginning, everything was perfect; everything was in the light, and God called it good.

Adam only had one rule – *"Don't eat of the tree of the Knowledge of Good and Evil."* Everything else in the garden was good for food. We all know that Eve was deceived by the devil in the form of a serpent. She was not seduced sexually by the snake as some have claimed, (the Bible does not teach that.) However, she was seduced with the knowledge; that if she would eat of this tree, she would become like God. Her decision, along with her husband's actions in following her lead, plunged the world into darkness. What was once lovely and good was now dark and dismal.

The first evidence they discovered in the darkness was that they were naked and ashamed. They didn't know what naked was until the veil of innocence dissolved from their lives. When God approached

1

them, they hid themselves because the feeling of shame was new to them and this feeling alarmed them. When God asked them about this new condition, they played the blame game. Adam blamed the woman and the woman blamed the serpent.

We hear this excuse a lot in today's society. Out of the 6, 840, 507, 000 people in the world today, there is someone putting the blame of their circumstances on someone else every second of the day. Whether the blame is placed on a group of people, on the government or their social disposition during childhood, someone else is going to be blamed for their position in life. One of first characteristics we see in the kingdom of darkness is the blame game.

This act of disobedience changed the lives of all three characters forever; it also changed the world.

The first judgment came against the serpent:

Genesis 3:14
Because you have done this, you are cursed more than all cattle, and more than every beast of the field; on your belly you shall go, and you shall eat dust all the days of your life.

So the serpent received a life-changing prophecy from God for his deception that changed the characteristics of the world. He would lose his legs and crawl on his belly for the rest of his life, eating the dust of the field. It is also a sign of extreme humiliation. It is no wonder why snakes are so creepy. The world's leading herpetologists agree that snakes used to have appendages, or legs. This particular reptile devolved into what they are today.

Genesis 3:15.
And I will put enmity between you and the woman, and between your seed and her Seed; He shall bruise your head, and you shall bruise His heel.

This is the first prophecy concerning the coming of the Messiah, which is Jesus the Christ. God said, "I will put enmity between you

2

and the woman." *Enmity* means, conflict. So this verse is telling us that there will be conflict between Satan's demons and God's children. There would be conflict between the children of light and the children of darkness. Her Seed represents Christ Jesus Who won the cosmic struggle over Satan and his associates.

When Adam ate of the tree of the Knowledge of Good and Evil, the world was plunged into darkness. Life as he knew it was not easy any longer because the ground was now cursed because of their sin. All things that were good devitalized into ungodly characteristics.

> *Genesis 3:17b-19*
> *Cursed is the ground for your sake; in toil you shall eat of it all the days of your life. Both thorns and thistles it shall bring forth for you, and you shall eat the herb of the field.*
> *In the sweat of your face you shall eat bread till you return to the ground, for out of it you were taken; for dust you are and to dust you shall return.*

Many people believe that this was for yesterday, but the truth of the matter is that this condition still exists today. We are still plowing the ground for food and vegetables. We are still dealing with thorns, thistles and nasty weeds. The people of the earth have been doing this since the fall of man. This consequence is still active in the world today. So from that point on, the people of the earth were born and lived in *chôshek*, or *darkness*. *Chôshek* is the Hebrew word for *darkness* and is defined as misery, destruction, death, ignorance, sorrow, wickedness, night and obscurity. In this darkness, we all were spiritually separated from God from birth.

The Great Fall

"You were the seal of perfection, full of wisdom and perfect in beauty. You were in Eden, the Garden of God; every precious stone was your covering: the sardius, topaz, and diamond, beryl, onyx, sapphire, turquoise, and emerald with gold."

This passage from *Ezekiel 28* depicts Lucifer's covering (or clothes) that were made of precious stones. We wear clothes made from animals and plants; like leather or silk or cotton. Lucifer wore cloths made of sardius, topaz, diamonds, gold and so on. His covering also suggests that he was high in the order of heavenly beings.

There are some who believe that the King of Tyre was actually a king that ruled back in the day. But there were only two people that were in the Garden of God (Garden of Eden) and they were Adam and Eve. But there's more:

> *"The workmanship of your timbrel and pipes was prepared for you on the day you were created."*

Lucifer is a created being. It seems that God took great care in creating him. The workmanship of musical instruments was imbedded in his body much like the organs (liver, lungs, stomach, kidneys etc…) of men are imbedded. The timbrel is an ancient percussion instrument that is similar to the tambourine, and pipes that are used in organs. Evidently, along with the precious jewels that made up his covering, Lucifer's body was a musical instrument; he was an embodiment of music.

When we look in The Book of the Revelation of Jesus Christ, chapter 4 verses 7-11, we get a picture of worship in heaven:

> *"The first living creature was like a lion, the second living creature like a calf, the third living creature had the face of a man, the fourth living creature was like a flying eagle. The four living creatures, each had six wings, were full of eyes around and within. And they do not rest day and night, saying: "Holy, Holy, Holy, Lord God Almighty, Who was and is and is too come!"*
> *"Whenever the living creatures gave glory and honor and thanks to Him Who sits on the throne, Who lives forever and ever, the twenty four elders fall down before Him Who sits on the throne and worship Him Who lives forever, and cast their crowns before the throne saying: "You are worthy O Lord, to*

receive glory and honor and power; for you created all things, and by You all things exist and were created."

It is evident that worship is an ongoing event in heaven, an eternal twenty-four hours a day, for an eternal seven days a week through an eternal fifty-two weeks a year. Day and night is the time for worship in heaven and Lucifer was created for worship. His body was created as a musical instrument to lead in worship to the One who sat on the throne. Lucifer led praise and worship before the throne of God.

The Bible records this in *Isaiah 14:12-14.*

"How you are fallen from heaven, O Lucifer, son of the morning! How you are cut down to the ground, you who weaken the nations! For you have said in your heart:
I will ascend into heaven,
I will exalt my throne above the stars of God,
I will also sit on the mountain of the congregation on the farthest sides of the north;
I will ascend above the heights of the clouds,
I will be like the most High."

This passage contains the origin of pride. *Pride, arrogance, vanity,* and *conceit* became a characteristic in Lucifer's mind during the eons of leading praise and worship. He wanted to be like God, he wanted to be worshipped as God and his thoughts betrayed him to God. *"How you are fallen from heaven, O Lucifer, son of the morning!"* In order to fall, you have to be elevated. He held a high position in heaven but his thought life cut him down to the ground.

"You who weaken the nations" is believed to be present, past and future. Satan has been interfering with human beings right after the beginning of time. He has influenced men to rebel against God, to turn their backs on God, to curse God and call God a liar by their actions; this will certainly weaken a nation.

Somehow, it got into Lucifer's mind that he could take over heaven and exalt himself above God, his Creator. *'I will exalt my throne above the stars of God.'* The stars in this passage of scripture and many other passages throughout the Bible are angels. The stars of God are the angels of heaven as noted in these scriptures.

Example:
Revelation 1:20b
The seven stars are the angels of the seven churches.

These seven stars are seven ministerial angels who are guardians over the churches.

Revelation 8:10-11a
Then the third angel sounded: and a great star fell from heaven burning like a torch, and it fell on a third of the rivers and on the springs of water. The name of the star is Wormwood.

We get a little information on the star in this passage. This one has a name, *Wormwood.* He must be a bitter or poisonous eternal being because when he touches the earth's springs of waters, they are poisoned and many men will die from the drinking water in these days to come.

Revelation 12:4a
His tail drew a third of the stars of heaven and threw them to the earth.

Here we see a third of the angelic beings captured in the deception of Satan and thrown down to the earth. These are the principalities, powers, rulers of darkness age, spiritual host of wickedness, and millions of evil spirits, and demon, and devils. The Bible says that his tail drew all these spiritual citizens of darkness on to the Earth. We will read more on this in the next chapter.

'The mountain of congregation is the heavenly Mount Zion." (See *Heb. 12:22)* Lucifer wanted to rule over the angels of heaven, he wanted to be recognized as the god over God. This is rebellion in the eyes of God. And as a result of his thoughts of rebellion and mental attempted hostile takeover, Lucifer was utterly cast down and lost his standing as an archangel of God. He lost his prestige as a cherub that covers, and became the devil.

It is a custom of God to change the name of someone. We see it when He changed the name of Abram to Abraham, the Father of many nations. We see it when He changed the name of Jacob the Cheater to Israel, the name that carries a nation. When he was the choir director in heaven, his name was Lucifer. When he rebelled against God, his name devolved to the title of: The Devil, or his character: The Serpent or The Dragon.

The Devil has a menu of names: He is the Accuser of the Brethren in *Revelation 12*; he is the Adversary in *1 Peter 5:8*; he is the Angel of the bottomless pit in *Revelation 9:11*; he is the God of this world in *2 Corinthians 4:4*; and he is a murderer in *John 8:44*. He is also called Abaddon, Apollyon, Beelzebub, Belial, Old Serpent, Prince of Demons, Ruler of Darkness and the Wicked One.

With the many names that he is identified with, it is no wonder that he is slanderous and fierce, deceitful and powerful, proud and cowardly and just plain wicked. Since his demise, he interferes in the lives of men by tricking those into doing his will. He possesses men by entering them and causing them to support his cause. He binds men with blindness, sickness and every other trouble under the sun. He has this power over his own children, people who have rejected God and His Christ.

For believers, he can only tempt us and try to afflict us. He accuses us to God and tries to sift us. He does his best to bring trouble to the children of God and if given the chance, he will. He looks for men that do not know who they are in Christ; he troubles them with his thoughts and deception and tries to make men turn away from God.

Ezekiel 28 reveals some things about the great enemy of mankind:

Ezekiel 28:14
"You were the anointed cherub who covers; I established you; you were on the mountain of God; you walked back and forth in the midst of the fiery stones. You were perfect in your ways from

the day you were created, till iniquity was found in you."

God established Lucifer Himself. He garnished his celestial body as an instrument of praise and worship and he was adorned with clothes of precious jewels and stones. He had the freedom to walk back and forth in the midst of fiery stones. God said he was perfect in his ways until *iniquity, heinousness, vice, immorality,* and *evil* was found in him.

> *Ezekiel 28:16-17*
> *"By the abundance of your trading you became filled with violence within, and you sinned. Therefore I cast you as a profane thing out of the mountain of God; and I destroyed you, O covering cherub, from the midst of the fiery stones. Your heart was lifted up because of your beauty; you corrupted your wisdom for the sake of your splendor; I cast you to the ground, I laid you before kings that they might gaze at you."*

Success ruined Lucifer in heaven; the abundance of his trading went to his head which gave birth to *pride, arrogance* and *conceit* with a touch of superiority. So God cast Lucifer out as a *profane, blasphemous, disrespectful* and *wicked thing* from Zion, which is His heavenly mountain.

Everything that God creates, the devil tries to destroy. If he can't destroy it, he will distort it, if he can't distort it, he will try to change it. For instance, the children of Israel sang songs to the Lord and praised Him for His mercy, His awesomeness, His grace, His power, His might, and His love. But at the same time, the nations that served false gods also sang to their gods of wood, stone, mud and whatever the works of their hands created. They sang songs to these demon gods as they sacrificed their flocks and children to appease them. These songs were generally driving songs that had repetitive lyrics that communicated with the souls of men and woman. These songs stirred the carnal passions, appealed to the souls of men and woman to the point of manipulation. By these demons of the underworld, songs, music and beats were authored, arranged and prepared to influence the people to do whatever they wanted them to do.

Daniel prophesied that in the last days, the Antichrist system would change times, laws and whatever else he could do to cause the people on the earth to *rebel* against God. And he has been very successful in music. Music has influenced people to *have sex* with one another, *assault* one another, *enrage* one another, *kill* one another, and *partake* in drugs with one another.

All music/songs are not evil music/songs; there are love songs, dance songs, songs of relationships and songs of wholesome fellowship. Music appeals to matters of the heart. There is music that brings joy to the hearts of men and there are songs that focus on the events of the day.

Today, Satan receives massive forms of worship through *secular music* which focuses on *sexual acts, carnal living,* which produces the *fruit of the flesh. Rebellious songs* are played over the air waves (remember he is the prince of the power of the air) that promotes *violence, homosexuality, hatred, adultery, sex outside of marriage, uncleanness, vulgarity, sorcery (which includes drug use), murder, heresies* and the *service to other gods.*

There are great musicians that drive these songs with rhythm and melody that makes an impact on the lives of men. Many who groove to the beats and the musical poetry do not realize they are listening to music that is *disrespectful* toward God.

Notes:

Chapter 2

What is Darkness?

There are basically two types of darkness that is mentioned in the New Testament. *Skotos* and *Scotia*. The first one is *Skotos* as represented in *Luke 11:34-35*:

> *The lamp of the body is the eye. Therefore when your eye is good, your whole body is full of light. But when your eye is bad, your body is also full of darkness. Therefore take heed that the light which is in you is not darkness.*

Our eyes and ears are the gates to our spirit, soul. When we spend time *reading* and/or *watching* wickedness, and *listening* to wickedness, then our lives will display wickedness. When we spend our time in the Word of God and working on our relationship with God, then our lives will also demonstrate it. You have heard the phrase, *"You are what you eat."* Whatever you *take in* through your portals will display who you are.

The local and national news report the outcome of what people have been *feeding on* every day. Each day there is a report of someone killing someone else. This person had been *accommodating* acts of murder through his/her *eye* and *ear gates* through meditation or rolling the act over and over in their minds. These people will roll the video in their minds over and over again until something triggers an action and the deed is done.

The entertainment world and the news media have a lot to do with *feeding the minds of the masses.* Millions of people *witness* several murders every hour in television shows and movies. *Rapes, chil-*

dren molestation, porn, thefts, violence, deception, unforgiveness, witch craft, sorcery, drug use, sex slaves, greed for material things, malice, lust for flesh, and many things that are not welcome in the Kingdom of God are *portrayed* over and over again by the entertainment media. When people watch this behavior over and over again, it becomes a *part of them* and most will *act it out* sooner or later. We are what our hearts feed on and these events happens because we have welcomed these activities through our *eye gates* and *ear gates*.

David said in *Psalms 101:3a, "I will set nothing wicked before my eyes."* What we do in private will set the stage of who we are in public. In other words, the time we spend in the works of darkness will manifest itself sooner or later.

Skotos - is defined as "to cover" The word is used literally for physical darkness and metaphorically for *spiritual, moral,* and *intellectual* darkness. This darkness arises out of *error, ignorance, disobedience, willful blindness* and *rebellion* against the truth of God's Word. Therefore, *darkness is an evil system* that is absolutely opposed to the light; or darkness is a system that is absolutely opposed to God for He is Light. It is a system that is absolutely opposed to the precepts of God. Satan wants to cover the world with *skotos* or darkness. Let's look at these traits of error a little closer.

Error is defined as:

1. An act, assertion, or belief that unintentionally deviates from what is correct, right, or true. The state of having false knowledge.
2. A deviation from an accepted code or behavior.
    a. Ignorant – Without knowledge or education.
    b. Displaying – Showing the lack of knowledge or education.
    c. Unaware or uninformed.
(1) Disobedience – Failure or refusal to obey
(2) Blindness – Being without sight - unable or unwilling to understand.
(3) Rebellion – An opening or organized opposition intended to change or overthrow an existing government or ruling

authority. (2) An act or show of defiance toward an authority or established convention.

Let's look at some examples of these types of darkness

In *Exodus 32*, we see an example of darkness. God *led* the children of Israel out of the land of Egypt through many signs and wonders; such as the ten plagues. God *caused* the people of Egypt to give the children of Israel all of their gold, silver, and precious stones. God *led* them with the pillar of fire by night and a cloud through the day. God *caused* Israel to escape through the Red Sea while the Egyptians drowned within minutes of their safe passage through the parted body of water. The acts of God were established. Every child of Israel knew that God had delivered them.

After all of this: Moses went to the Mountain of God and was there for 40 days.

Now when the people saw that Moses delayed coming down from the mountain, the people gathered together to Aaron, and said to him, *"Come, make us gods that shall go before us; for as for this Moses, the man who brought us out of the land of Egypt, we do not know what happened to him."*

The kingdom of darkness does not have the ability to possess patience. Remember every person born after the fall of Adam and Eve were born with a sin nature. They knew of God, but they didn't really know God. Through *spiritual error*, they claimed that Moses led them out of Egypt and then disappeared upon the Mountain of God. The acts of God did not sink in because they had been *brainwashed for years* and needed something tangible they could see. They couldn't see God, so they *could not follow God due to error*, which lead to *spiritual blindness*, and *rebellion*.

The kingdom of darkness had an *effect* on the people. 40 days after God had delivered the people of Israel, they decided to *make another god* to follow. The Scriptures go on to say in *Exodus 32* that Aaron the priest, Moses' brother, collected the gold, silver and precious stones to fashion a golden calf to worship. The children of Israel *deviated* from serving the God that delivered them from the hands of Egypt, and were *enticed* to make another god to follow. God had shown them His attributes and His power when He delivered them. But they *did not honor* Him as God but *forsook* Him and *made for themselves* another god that is not God at all. This is error and rebellion. The children deviated from God's accepted code of behavior. But thank God for His mercy.

To live in error is truly a terrible thing. Error can and will lead a person *down a road* in such a *mental state of confusion* that the person will *not have a clue of the danger* they are in. It is like driving down the road at 120 mph and the bridge is out up ahead. The sign tells you that the bridge is out, but you *don't believe* that the sign is true. So the person *continues on* until the reality of gravity becomes apparent in his or her life. Another example of this is men who believe in their hearts that they were born to be women and vice versa. This belief is so *deeply felt* that extreme measures of surgeries are taken to accomplish this task and to fulfill *their belief system*. So they continue to *live under* this *falsehood*. This is living in darkness, living in error.

The Jews also operated in error. They hung their hopes on the coming Messiah. They believe that the Messiah would come and wipe out the Romans and establish His reign upon the earth. But when Jesus the Messiah stood before them, taught before them and showed signs that God was working through Him to heal and to perform miracles, they *did not accept* Him. They said they were Moses' disciples, but the reality is; Moses hung his hopes on the coming Christ that is 'Christ Jesus, the hope of glory.' Jesus pointed this out in *John 5:46*.

For if you believe Moses, you would believe Me; for he wrote about Me. But if you do not believe his writings, how will you believe My words?

Another example of error is found in Christian circles in which one group of people believes in certain parts of the bible. For instance, some Christian folks believe miracles are a thing of the past or outdated. They even give *their* belief a name – But God calls it *doubt* and *unbelief*. In addition, some Christians believe that the spiritual gifts, listed in The Book of 1st Corinthians are of the devil; this is error. God gave these gifts so that His Church would be healthy and vibrant that will win many souls to the Lord. Error is *a tool* of darkness designed to *bring separation* to the body of Christ and to keep the Christian man and woman *ignorant* and *non-effective* in life.

Being *erroneous* or *inaccurate* in the Word of God is a major, major problem in the some churches today. Some churches have developed a complex of a *self-made god*. Meaning, we develop a Jesus, or Savior, through *selected* Scriptures that *we like*. Or we like using partial Scriptures to fulfill the promises of God. For instances in *James 4:7* it says:

> *Therefore submit to God. Resist the devil and he will flee from you.*

Folks love the idea of the devil fleeing from them however; he will not flee unless you are submitted to God. If a Christian man or woman is not submitting to God, then the devil has no reason to flee.

People want the devil to flee *without following the rules.* Submitting to God should be first and foremost in our daily walk and the only way the devil will flee from you is because you are submitted to God. He will not flee when a person is not in the attitude of submission to the Lord. The *Book of Acts* tells a story of seven sons of a Jewish Priest named Sceva. These seven sons tried to cast out a demon and the demon answered, *'Jesus I know, Paul I know, but who are you?'* Then the demon beat the clothes off of the seven sons of Sceva. If you do not have the greater One in you, the devil has no reason to be afraid of you and has no reason to flee. So when the person tells the devil to flee without submitting to God, the darkness will stand up and suggest something like this to the uncommitted one, 'God doesn't love you or care about you,' or 'this stuff don't work on me.' Most likely the person will get mad at God or call Him a liar because they believe that His Word didn't work for them. A lot of people think that the Word works but it won't work for them because they have committed some sin, or they are not worthy of deliverance from the evil one. When in all actuality, it did not work because we *refused to submit to God.*

Draw near to God and He will draw near to you

This is why it is vital to have a relationship with God. If you do not seek Him, you simply will not find Him. The Scripture tells us to seek the Lord while He may be found. This suggests that there will come a time when He will not be found. *Isaiah 55:6.* Jesus tells us to *seek ye first the Kingdom of God in Matthew 6:33, and all these things shall be added to you;* and in *Matthew 7:7 it tells us that when we seek and we shall find.* However, some people do not want to seek, but they want to receive the things of God without any effort in seeking God or submitting to God.

Another popular Scripture is found in *Mark 11:23 and 24* where Jesus tells us to have the God-kind of faith, and if you believe, you will be able to speak to things that are in your life and they will be removed. Everyone loves that part of the scripture. But *Mark 11:25,* tells us that if we do not have forgiveness in our hearts God will not forgive our sins and trespasses. When we have unforgiveness in our hearts, we cannot get our prayers answered. We cannot have the one without the other.

Today's equivalent; is trying to drive your car without having gas in your tank. You must deposit gasoline in your tank and then you will be able to drive your car anywhere you wish. Therefore, when we look at the Scriptures, we must look at the entire Scripture in order for them to be fulfilled in our own lives. So when we obey the entire Word of God, we are fine. When we don't, then we are in *disobedience* and *fall into error* because we are not following the full instruction. Remember King Saul. When we are partial in Scriptures then we are in essence, *serving another jesus* and this *'jesus'* will be a self-conjured deity. Or to put it plainly, it would be *another jesus, a different jesus than the one in the Bible.*

In *Galatians 1*, Paul warns us about serving *a different jesus, a different gospel* than the true one.

Galatians 1:6-8
I marvel that you are turning away so soon from Him Who called you in the grace of Christ, to a different gospel, which is

16

not another; but there are some who trouble you and want to pervert the gospel of Christ. But even if we, or an angel from heaven, preach any other gospel to you than what we preached to you, let him be accused.

Notes:

Chapter 3

Spiritual Error

Another biblical example of spiritual error is the encounter of Jesus and the Sadducees. The story is recorded in *Matthew 22, Mark 12*, and in *Luke 20*.

> *Luke 20:27-38*
> *Then some of the Sadducees, who deny that there's a resurrection, came to Jesus and asked Him, saying "Teacher, Moses wrote to us that if a man's brother dies, having a wife, and he dies without children, his brother should take his wife and raise up offspring for his brother.*
>
> *Now there were seven brothers. And the first took a wife, and died without children.*
>
> *And the second took her as wife, and he died childless. Then the third took her, and in like manner the seventh also; and they left no children, and died. Last of all, the woman died also.*
>
> *Therefore, in the resurrection, whose wife does she become? For all seven had her as wife."*
>
> *Jesus answered and said to them, 'The sons of this age marry and are given in marriage. But those who are counted worthy to attain that age, and the resurrection from the dead, neither marry nor are given in marriage; nor can they die anymore, for they are equal to the angels and are sons of God, being sons of the resurrection.*
>
> *But even Moses showed in the burning bush passage that the dead are raised, when he called the Lord the God of Abraham, the God of Isaac, and the God of Jacob.'" For He is not the God*

of the dead but of the living, for all live to Him.

This is one of the strangest passages in the Bible, but it clearly shows that darkness had *clouded* the minds of the Sadducees. As a group, they *did not believe* in the resurrection. They believed this present life was all there was. They *assumed* there wasn't any form of existence, or life after death.

The Sadducees asked Jesus about the conditions of marital status in heaven, after death. The state of darkness had them so *encompassed with deception*; they asked Jesus a question about a condition that they *did not believe in.*

However, the true quest of the Sadducees was to corner the Son God into saying something against the teachings of Moses so that they could *trap* Him and *accuse* Him of heresy or blasphemy. However, we can see the power of darkness in their *minds* and *hearts* because their *intentions* were wrapped in deception. *Satan was behind the actions* here because he wanted to cause Jesus to stumble in response to God's doctrine, or the ways of God. **Darkness cannot overcome the light – the light will always overcome the darkness.**

Notes:

Chapter 4

Ignorance

Hosea 4:6a
My people are destroyed for lack of knowledge...

 Ignorance is the condition of being *uneducated, unaware* or *uninformed.* In spiritual matters, some people are ignorant of the ways of the spirit because of their location. Tribal people are ignorant of the salvation in Christ and the Kingdom of God because no one has reached them preaching and sharing the Word of God. There have been many, many missionaries that I am aware of that have covered a great deal of isolated places. Wayne and Dayne Sanders of Common Ground Ministries go to Honduras and minister to the people there every year. Brother Daryl of Open Skies Ministries packed up his belongings and preached the Gospel in the Philippines. He then settled down in Doha, Qatar, built a church there and has been doing the work of the Gospel ever since. Then there are people like Pastors Billy Joe and Sharon Daugherty of Victory Christian Center, who take frequent trips to Africa, South America, Russia and other places to share the Gospel of God's love. And then there is Smith Wigglesworth who went everywhere the Lord called him to go. These are just a few, but there are many, many ministries who are going into the places where people have never heard of the Lord Jesus Christ and they are preaching the Gospel to them so they may receive eternal life.

Romans 16:14
How then shall they call on Him in whom they have not be-

lieved? And how shall they believe in Him of whom they have not heard? And how shall they hear without a preacher?

It takes ministers of righteousness to go into the darkness as Jesus and His disciples did to proclaim the Kingdom of God is at hand. These ministers of righteousness shed light on the true life that God has ordained for us to live in. If the light is not shed, then people will remain in darkness.

> *Romans 10:15-17*
> *And how shall they preach unless they are sent? As it is written: How beautiful are the feet of those who preach the gospel of peace, who bring glad tidings of good things. But they have not all obeyed the gospel. For Isaiah says, 'Who has believed our report?' So then faith comes by hearing and hearing by the word of God.*

The purpose of the five-fold ministry is to preach and teach the Word of God. The purpose is to minister to the lost folks in their current condition, and shed the light of the truth of God so they may receive understanding. When this is done, the people should no longer be ignorant of the Gospel of Christ. When light is applied, darkness fades away.

However, there are people who have the opportunity to hear the Gospel preached so that they may receive eternal life. Unfortunately, they *refuse* the Gospel for some *fleshly* or *carnal reason* or another and will literally *choose* to stay in the darkness. God says that His wrath is on those who do not believe that Jesus is the Son of God *(See Rom. 1:18; Jo. 3:36).* Then we have people who go to church every Sunday, hear the sermon, (not Listen to the sermon), and leave on the same spiritual level as they were when they went to the service. These folks *do not want change* in their lives because *the darkness is comfortable to them.* This is *willful ignorance* because they *do not want to hear the truth* so that their lives can change.

Chapter 5

Disobedience

Disobedience is a *refusal* or a *failure* to obey. The classic tale of disobedience is found in the Book of Genesis. Adam and Eve had simple instructions; they could eat from any tree in the garden except for the tree of the Knowledge of Good and Evil. As you know, they disobeyed God and the world has been suffering ever since.

While they obeyed the Lord God, the world was fine, but when Eve was *tricked* by the dark lord and decided to *eat from the forbidden* tree, and Adam ate of it also – the world was *plunged* into darkness, into his playing field, and into *his arena*. There is a reason God gives us instructions. The reason is basically to protect us and to keep us in His arena, or under the wings of the Almighty, *Psalm 91:1*. We truly do not have a clue to all the spiritual things that are happening, including the *spiritual warfare* that is going go all around us. Most Christians *haven't a clue to the demonic activity* in the world and even in own their lives. For some, it is these same demonic *entities* in which they *do not believe* in, are the very same demonic entities that are *wreaking havoc* in their lives. Walking by faith and not by sight hasn't been revealed to most of the churches, mainly because she has *refused* or *chose to ignore* God's instruction. The reason for this is mainly because of the *other doctrines*, (a different jesus'), which has *polluted* the church houses across the nation and around the globe.

This is not to say all churches are in disobedience. There are several hundred, if not thousands of churches that cling to the doctrine of Christ and live in obedience to His Word. We just have to find them and join the good fight of faith.

Another classic tale of disobedience is the story of Saul, the first king of Israel. In the Book of *1 Samuel 15:3*, Saul was told by the prophet of God, Samuel, to kill all the Amalekites, every man, woman, child, ox, sheep, camel and donkey. God wanted to punish them for the attitude they displayed when Israel came out of Egypt. And He wanted to use the army of Israel to wipe the entire nation off the face of the earth.

But Saul only *partially obeyed* the word from the Lord and even though he killed all the people, he was *unwilling* to kill the king and to top it off; he saved the best of the animals. Why? One, he *disobeyed* mainly because he feared men more than he feared God. And two, he wanted to please the men that had fought with him. And somehow, he got an idea that God would be okay with his compromise. Saul *did not know* God very well. He *didn't understand* that God had a purpose for the annihilation of the Amalekites. He didn't understand that it is very important to follow His instructions to the T for *the smallest thing* can lead a leader into disaster.

Either we are obedient or we are not. My favorite example is that a woman is either pregnant or she is not. She can't be halfway pregnant or almost pregnant, either she is or she isn't. This is also true in the Word of God; there isn't any *middle ground* or *gray area* in the ways of God. There is no such thing as a *part time* believer and there is no such thing as *partial* obedience. James gave a wonderful illustration when he said, *"Does a spring send forth fresh water and bitter water from the same opening." - James 3:11.* Likewise we are either obedient or we are not. We are either faithful to God or we are not. We either love Him or we don't.

Partial disobedience is still disobedience. It is like building a house; you lay the foundation, put up the dry wall, and install the pluming without grafting into the sewage or the water system. You run the electrical lines, but you don't hook them into the power source. The setup is there, but it *won't function* until the entire task is completed.

I want to take a little time to think about the 'what ifs'. What if the children of Israel didn't follow God's instruction and walk around Jericho for the days required in silence and shout on the last

24

day? Would Israel have the victory that they had that day? If Naaman had not dipped himself in the Jordan River seven times, would he have been healed of his leprosy? What if the woman in Elijah's time ate the food first and offer the last to the prophet, do you think the results would have been the same. What if Jesus got on the cross but had not died for our sins in order to purchase a place for us in heaven. What if he only paid half the price for our sins and we had to pay the other half. Would we be the righteousness of God in Christ Jesus today? Jesus was *obedient* in all points and was found *faultless*. If He was partially obedient then we would not have a chance for eternal life. We would still be wallowing in the mire of sin and citizens in the kingdom of darkness.

King Saul was obedient in *only part* of the task God had told him to do, to kill everything. However, he *didn't complete* the mission. He only *completed part* of the task. Because of Saul's disobedience, God *rejected* him as king of Israel and began grooming David to take his place. David was a man after God's own heart.

As we have determined, *disobedience* is a *refusal* or a *failure* to obey. It is also not following the instructions of the Lord exactly. In *Numbers 20*, we find the children of Israel complaining against Moses again on a water shortage issue. At this point, Moses had grown weary in his constant intercession for the peoples' *complaints* and *comments* about going back to Egypt. God told Moses to speak to the rock and it will bring forth water. However, Moses was a little testy that day and he struck the rock, (I believe out of frustration), and it produced the same results as before. In *Verse 12*, the Lord God said Moses had *unbelief* in Him and therefore Moses was *disqualified* from entering into the promise land. This may seem harsh to some, but God is setting an example for us to live by. We must be obedient to His Word.

Partial disobedience is still disobedience. God's Word is to be followed explicitly. If God says speak to the rock, then we must speak to the rock. If God says give the homeless man a hundred dollar bill then we should give the homeless man a hundred dollar bill, not a twenty, or a fifty, but the hundred. However, many people *have a problem* with the Word of the Lord. The reason for this is because these same people walk according to their flesh and not according to the Spirit. They are not thinking about the will of God, their thoughts are in self-preservation. *(See Rom. 8:1-11)* For instance, God tells us that we must love (agapē) our brothers. God is talking about loving our brothers and sisters unconditionally, as He loves us. This means, when a brother or a sister in the Lord offends you or gets under your skin, we are to love them regardless of what they have done to us.

Some won't love because a person has stolen something from them and they can't forgive. It may be money, an item, or even a spouse. Some can't forgive because of difference of opinions. Some cannot love because of prejudice, bigotry or some other carnal reason. We have to find a way to get away from this stinkin' thinkin' and the only way to do that is to give your life to Christ and let the Holy Spirit clean you up.

> *Matthew 5:43-48*
> *You have heard that it was said, 'You shall love your neighbor and hate your enemy.' But I say to you, love your enemies, bless those who curse you, do good to those who hate you, and pray for those who spitefully use you and persecute you, that you may be sons of your Father in heaven; for He makes His sun rise on the evil and on the good, and sends rain on the just and on the unjust.*
>
> *For if you love those who love you, what reward have you? Do not even the tax collectors do the same?*
>
> *And if you greet your brethren only, what do you do more than others? Do not even the tax collectors do so? Therefore you shall be perfect, just as your Father in heaven is perfect.*

Love your enemies, bless those who curse you, do good to those who hate you, and pray for those who spitefully use you. This is agape. This is unconditional love. A love that does not seek revenge, does not take offense, but it operates from a pure heart. A heart full of forgiveness is the very kind of heart every Christian must live in.

The world often confuses *agapē* (unconditional love), with *philĕō* (brotherly love) and/or *ĕrŏs'*(sensual love). *Agapē* is God's kind of love and it is unconditional. This means God loves us no matter what. *Philĕō* is a brotherly love we should share with others. *Ĕrŏs'* is a sensual love, it the root word in which we get the word *'erotica'* and this type of love should only be shared with your husband or wife.

We should never get these words confused as some have done already. Believing that we are to have love *(Ĕrŏs')* for our brothers and sisters in a sexual manner is a serious error. *Ĕrŏs'* is a love that is shared between you and your spouse. This confusion was not God's intention for us; it is an example of the darkness perverting the Word of God. The darkness loves to obfuscate the difference between God's *agapē* and *philĕō* and *ĕrŏs'*.

The Lord told us in John 15, we are to love one another and in *1 John 4:20 He asks, how can we love God whom we have never seen and not our brothers who we see every day.* So when we do not love our brother for denominational issues, racial issues, gender issues, or what-so-ever issues, we are in disobedience. God has commanded us to love our neighbors and our brothers. But some of us do not like, much less love our brothers and sisters for some silly reason or another. So we find ways to get around obeying the Word of God. Darkness will always *create excuses* to *get around* the word of God.

Another example of disobedience is *the great commission* listed in *Mark 16* and *Matthew 28*. The commission is not just for the leaders in the church, it is for *all* believers. It is not just the leaders who are to go and spread the Gospel. It is also the *responsibility* of the believers to spread the Gospel of Christ. We are to be *witnesses* for Christ. We are to be witnesses in our conversation, our attitudes, and in our general way of life. Jesus tells us, if we are ashamed of Him, then He will be ashamed of us in the presence of the Father *(See Mk. 8:38)*. When we understand in the Word that we are to spread the Gospel and we *decide not to*, or decide that this is not my calling – we will understand on that day that this is disobedience. We must be obedient to the Word of God. When we don't, *we invite* darkness into our lives.

The best way to be witness for Christ is to tell others what Jesus has done for you. This makes your testimony close and personal. An example is, "I was a whoremonger, a thief, a drug addict, a chronic liar and I called on Christ and He saved me, He changed my life." This is the best tool to be witnesses for Christ – to *tell others* what He did in our lives.

The purpose of the Great Commission is for those who have had an encounter with God to share with those who have not had an encounter with God. God knows who will accept Him and He knows who will reject Him. We do not know who will accept Him or who will reject Him, but we must go to everyone the Holy Spirit sends us to.

> *John 1:12*
> *And for those who accept Christ as Lord and Savior, to them he gave the right to become His children.*

Notes:

Chapter 6

Blindness

Blindness is also a result of error and is a *characteristic* of darkness. This is a hard and difficult fact to explain but it is the truth nonetheless. In the 9th chapter of John we find an interesting story of *spiritual blindness*. In the previous chapter, Jesus explained the difference between the children of God and the children of the devil. He illustrated the difference between the ways of Abraham's descendants and the ways of the devil's descendants. The Jews thought just "because they were of the linage of Abraham," they had an automatic ticket to paradise. But Jesus told them they were the sons of Satan because, they acted like Satan. The truth hurt them and they wanted to kill Him (which proved the point to be true) but Jesus walked right through the midst of them.

After He walked through the midst of the *murderous hearted* Jews, He saw a man who had been born blind. I want you to notice the presence of mind in Christ; although the Jews wanted to *kill* him, He still had the presence of mind to see a need for healing even when it seemed His own life was in danger. The darkness will always try to *divert* the Christian from his primary mission with *distractions* in one form or another. Darkness will always try to *distract* the brother or sister in Christ in order to *foil, hinder,* or *disrupt* the progress of the kingdom. Jesus came to seek and save that which is lost, to perform cures, heal the sick, raise the dead, and preach the kingdom of God. If Jesus had been affected by the threats of the Jews or anyone else, He probably would have passed right by the man born blind and *missed the opportunity* to demonstrate the power, love and compassion of the Kingdom of God.

The aspiration of the darkness is to get the Christian man or woman to *focus on the trap* which can cause us to *miss an opportunity* for the power of God to be manifested in the life of a hurting soul. I have experienced many times when I was either reading the Word, preparing a sermon, in quiet meditation, or even writing this book, someone will come to disrupt the flow. I don't believe they are doing this purposely, and yet it is still a common occurrence in the lives of men and women of God. Distractions will come. Jesus demonstrated even when distractions came, we still have a mission to do. God gives us the grace, "a divine influence upon the heart, and its reflection in the life. He gives us the *grace,* or *ability to handle* the diversion and to continue on with God's plan for mankind.

A young man came to see me one day and he had a problem. I was about18 months old in the Lord and I was reading and in prayer. I didn't want to be disturbed so I told the young man we would visit that evening. The young man went to work and killed another man. When I heard what happened, the Spirit of God was all over me because my *priorities* were not right. People need *help* and like Jesus, *we are to minister* to those who need help and not put them off.

When Jesus face was set toward Jerusalem, *(See Lk. 9:51)* first the Samaritan village rejected Him, and then His disciples wanted fire from heaven to consume the village. However, Jesus addressed the issues and went on His way. He did not belittle the situation or ignore it, He handled it. Jesus had a date with destiny and distractions were coming from the village and His disciples. If the darkness can get you to take your mind off of your mission, then he will use whatever is necessary to accomplish that goal, even if it is the people closest to you.

Let's get back to the man who was born blind. The disciples asked Jesus if the blindness was the result of the sin of the man or the sins of the parents. Jesus replied neither the man nor his parent's sins were the cause of the blindness. In those days, any ailments like blindness, deafness, or bodies that did not function as they were meant to function were considered a result of sin. However, Jesus said *this man was born blind so that the glory of God can be made manifest in him (or shown in him).* This man had lived in darkness all of his life and God was going to reveal Himself in the healing, (works of God), of the man born blind.

John 9:4-5
I must work the works of Him who sent Me while it is day; the night is coming when no one can work. As long as I am in the world, I am the light of the world.

'Works,' here is described as toil, occupation, enterprise, deed, task, accomplishment, employment, performance, labor or course of action. The Greek word for *works* is *'ergon'* and the word is compared to: 'energy and urge'. (See Strong's Exhaustive Concordance #2041)

Jesus is teaching His disciples that He had a *limited time* to be here on the earth, or in the world. So while He is here, He must do the work God the Father had sent Him do. *Sickness, disease* and *death* are the *symptoms* of *fallen* man. These *symptoms are the tools* of darkness to *discredit* God, but Jesus is showing Himself as an example of God's sovereignty and mercy in overcoming *the works* of darkness. This example is for us – today's church.

"*As long as I am in the world, I am the light of the world,*" Jesus said to them. Jesus was teaching His disciples He was on the earth to illuminate the ways of God. Jesus' mission was to bring *healing, deliverance* and *salvation* to the lost souls of the earth. His mission on the earth was to *expose* the darkness and *deliver* those who are bound in darkness by showing the *sovereignty, grace, power* and *mercy* of God the Father.

John 8:12
I am the light of the world. He who follows Me shall not walk in darkness, but have the light if life.

As the sun and moon gives physical light to the earth, Jesus came to *expose* sin and *give* spiritual sight as the light of the world. Jesus came to *set* a new order and He represented this new order as an example of a new creation and in Him was the Light of Life. The light of life is the wisdom of God, which is eternal life.

31

Colossians 1:13-14
He has delivered us from the power of darkness and con-
veyed us into the kingdom of the Son of His love, in whom we
have redemption through His blood, the forgiveness of sins.

In *John 9*, Jesus was setting the stage for *deliverance* out of the kingdom of darkness, *deliverance* from sickness, *deliverance* from disease, *deliverance* from the wiles of Satan, *deliverance* from hell and the pit of fire and brimstone. He came to destroy the hooks of sin in the mouths of men and women. The light destroys darkness. Not only are we *delivered* from these things but also, we have been placed in the family of God. For those who have faith in Him; by believing Him and following Him, these people have received the very nature of God. The nature of His love, the nature of His joy, the nature of everything He is; we are.

1 John 4:17
Love has been perfected among us in this: that we may have
boldness in the day of judgment; because as He is, so are we in
this world.

Jesus was giving the disciples a preliminary teaching through demonstration about the power of God that will dwell in them. He was laying the groundwork for the disciples to follow after they discover who they were in Christ Jesus, on the Day of Pentecost.

Chapter 7

Blindness continued

After the man who was born blind was healed, there was a ruckus about the city. They saw the newly healed man walking around praising God for his sight. It seemed everyone knew him, for he had been a planted fixture in the city for all of his life. I imagine he had spent his entire life before this gate or that gate, where the citizens of Jerusalem passed by him on a daily basis. However, on this day, something was different, the man they had passed by for years had changed. There was something different about him. He was no longer *blind* and *limited*, he was *healed* and *free*.

When a person has an encounter with God, there is a change. Some of the folks wondered, "Is this the man who was born blind? How is it he can see?" While others said, "Yes this is the blind man!" The man was formally blind, *declared with joy* he was the man born blind and *gave the testimony*; Jesus healed him. He had been *delivered from darkness* and he *rejoiced in the light*. He told them how Jesus made clay, anointed his eyes and told him to wash in the pool of '*Siloam*'; which means *sent*.

However, everyone was not happy with the healing. Why? It was because the healing took place on the Sabbath; the Pharisees were upset over the ordeal and proclaimed Jesus was not of God because He performed miracles on the Sabbath. The Jews had a thing about the Sabbath. God called the Sabbath a day of rest but the darkness had *twisted* the true meaning of God's intentions. God expects us to do good every day, including the Sabbath. Even today when my Jewish friends fast, they feel they are forbidden to use a remote control to change the television channel or turn it off. However, it is allowed to place a towel or a cloth over the television. What is the difference between the two? In the passage above, the Jews *disbelieved* Jesus had healed the man who was born blind and they were looking for *any excuse* to *discredit* Him.

Especially in the Gospels, we often see a sharp rebuke for religious folks who do not believe, but *performed as if* they were. When a person disbelieves God, the person *sets himself/herself on* a downward spiral toward the darkness. *2nd Thessalonians 2:11* tells us, when a person doesn't love the truth, (and embraces a lie), *God will give them a strong delusion to believe the lie.* In all actuality, God is giving the people *what they want.* When the Pharisees *doubted* and *disbelieved* the healing power of God working through Jesus, it caused them to be *spiritually blinded* by the fact something that has never been done in the history of the earth was done in their midst. They *saw it,* but they *couldn't see it.* This can be compared to the alcoholic/drug addict who says they are fine, "There is nothing wrong with me!" But deep within them they know they are tore up from the floor up. This is a true attribute of darkness. Doubt and unbelief will *deceive* you into thinking you are all right, even when you see your life spiraling down the tubes to destruction. Here they saw a miracle that had never happened in the history of man and one so powerful only God could have performed it; but they did not want to accept it and *the choice* of non-acceptance kept them in spiritual blindness.

The Jews were *offended* because this miraculous healing was done on the Sabbath, which incidentally, is a day to do good for another. *Offense* is a powerful tool used in the kingdom of darkness. *Offense* can cause a person to be steadfast in *unbelief, unforgiveness, stubbornness* and a host of other qualities not conducive to holy living. *Offense* can and will cause a person to stand for something wrong, even when the person knows that this is wrong – they will not budge on their stance. The Jewish leaders witnessed Jesus continually doing the works of the Kingdom of God, the Kingdom of Light but they *refused to receive* the truth.

So a debate broke out, some people believed Jesus was from God because of the healing power He demonstrated. Others said He was a sinner because He worked, or performed a miracle on a holy day. There will always be *a struggle* between light and darkness as God declared in Genesis 3 when He said, "

> *Genesis 3:15*
> *And I will put enmity between you and the woman, and between your seed and her Seed; He shall bruise your head, and you shall bruise His heel,"*

There will always be *a dispute* on spiritual matters between the children of light and the children of darkness.

The Pharisees began *questioning* the man about his healing but they *didn't believe* his story. They didn't believe his story because the outcome of the story was one they *did not want to hear*. They had *formed an opinion* about Jesus and the story was a contradiction to the opinion they had formed. They sought a second opinion and called his parents to the council and asked them. The parents confirmed he was born blind but *they didn't know* how their son was healed. They told the council to ask the son because he was of age.

The son repeated the testimony of his healing and the reply from the Pharisees was, "Give God the glory! We know this man (Jesus) is a sinner." It is a shame a miracle can stare you in the face, but because you operate in the ways of darkness, you become blind to the attributes and characteristics of God. The darkness will always take you *a step further in defiance* against God.

The man answered and he seemed to be a little peeved about the line of questioning. I believe it did not make any sense to him as to why they were acting this way. *"I told you already and you did not listen. Why do you want to hear it again?"* Reader, remember that *confusion* will always be present when the works of darkness is in operation. I believe the purpose of the Pharisees badgering the formally blind man was to get him to recant his story. I also believe if an opportunity had arisen, the Pharisees would attempt to *grab, take,* or *seize* the glory for the man's healing. So they were trying to *apply pressure* on him in order for him to change his story. Their tactics had already worked on the man's parents because they deflected the line of questioning to their son. You see the Pharisees had *threatened to excommunicate* anyone who confessed Jesus was the Christ. So if anyone didn't believe as they believed, they would be *thrown out* of the synagogue. Therefore, in order to save face, so to speak, the Pharisees needed to get the man to *deny* the fact Jesus performed a great and powerful miracle in his life.

"All I know" said the man who was formally blind, "I was blind and now I see." Then to pour gasoline on top of a fiery situation, the now seeing man asked, "Do you want to be His disciple?"

The *indignant* religious leaders exclaimed, "We are disciples of Moses and *we don't know* where this Jesus fella is from."

>John 5:39-40
>*You searched the scriptures, for in them you think you have eternal life; and these are they which testify of Me. But you are not willing to come to Me that you may life.*

These men had studied the Scriptures for most of their lives, but they only understood them from a *carnal nature* at best. The darkness had *blinded* them so badly that they *couldn't see* the truth was standing in front of them. You see, they had been looking for the Messiah for all of their years. They read and studied the prophecies of Isaiah, Psalms, Jeremiah, Malachi and others. They read the Words but the words weren't life to them. Why? Because they were *abiding in the darkness* and they were *comfortable in their carnality.* Why were they abiding in the darkness? It was because of their unbelief in Jesus being the Christ; the result of unbelief is darkness. The Jews knew Isaiah 61 and saw Jesus perform Isaiah 61 in front of them but *instead of* being joyful that the Son of God was in their midst, they *were offended.* They were also *offended* because Jesus didn't go to their schools nor did He get His knowledge from them. Imagine that, they wanted God in the flesh to go to their school and be taught by them.

I do not receive honor from men. But I know you, you do not have the love of God in you. I have come in My Father's Name, and you do not receive Me; if another comes in his name, him you will receive. How can you believe, who *receive honor from one another*, and do not seek the honor which only comes from God?

Snakes get along with snakes, pigs get along with pigs, and *birds of the feather flock together*. Religious men and women love the praise from other religious men and women. When a religious person rejects the teachings of Christ, they leave *a crack in the door* for the darkness to *creep into* their minds, establishing dark thoughts, which will turn into dark actions. In order to *appease* and be appeased, these individuals will encourage one another in their doomed plight for righteousness that only leads to *self-righteousness*. God says our righteousness is as filthy rags – in today's vernacular, 'our righteousness is as a used tampex/kotex.'

> *"Do not think that I shall accuse you to the Father, there is one who accuses you – Moses, in whom you trust. For if you believed Moses, you would believe Me; for he wrote about Me. But if you do not believe his writings, how will you believe My words?"*

The Jewish leaders trusted in Moses. They trusted in the words of Moses. However, they only trusted in him as a historical figure, and not as the prophet of God. For if they believed Moses prophesied about the Christ, they would have seen the Scriptures they trusted in were being fulfilled in the person of Jesus of Nazareth. With this revelation, they would have accepted Jesus as the Christ and would have come out of the darkness. But they didn't. I believe if they had been with Moses they would have rebelled against him just as Dathan and Korah had rebelled. The darkness is no respecter of persons. Satan will use whosoever to do his bidding. He will use anyone whose heart is not fixed on God. He will also use anyone who dabbles with the Word of God.

Jesus told them, if they believed Moses, they would believe Him because it was Jesus Moses was prophesying about. This statement was a fact, but the Jews *didn't receive it* as fact. Their *self-imposed blindness* kept them from believing.

Deuteronomy 18:18

I will raise up for them a Prophet like you from among their brethren, and I will put my words in His mouth, and He shall speak to them all that I command Him. And it shall be that whoever will not hear My words, which He speaks in My name, I will require it of him.

There were many bonafide prophets, who came after Moses, but this prophecy was talking about Jesus and Jesus fulfilled that prophecy. The prophecy says Jesus would speak God's Words. And Jesus Himself proclaimed He only spoke the Father's Words and even that didn't ring a bell. The scary part of the Scripture is when *they didn't believe* Him, God would require it of them. That means everyone who hears the Word of God is expected to act on the Word of God. When a person doesn't act on what they heard from God, they will have to *answer to God* for their actions, or non-action. It is not a good thing to disbelieve God, and all who do not line up with God's instruction are destined for the Lake of Fire.

We can see the transformation in the man who was formally blind. Not only was he healed physically, he was also healed spiritually and received revelation knowledge this man, Jesus, was from God.

John 9:30-33

The man answered and said to them, "Why, this is a marvelous thing, that you do not know where He is from; yet He has opened my eyes! Now we know that God does not hear sinners; but if anyone is a worshipper of God and does His will, He hears him. Since the world began it has been unheard of that anyone opened the eyes of one who was born blind. If this man were not from God He could do nothing."

After they threw the man out of the synagogue, Jesus found him and asked, "Do you believe in the Son of God?" The man *believed* and *worshipped* Him. He was happy and elated to be out of the physical darkness that hindered him all his life. He was happy Jesus the

Christ chose him to be an example of the *grace, love, goodness,* and *mercy* of God. It is wonderful for a person to be made an example of *the glory* of God as the man who was formally blind.

> *John 9:39-41*
> *And Jesus said, "For judgment I have come into this world, that those who do not see may see, and that those who see may be blind."*
>
> *Then some of the Pharisees who were with Him heard these words, and said to Him, "Are we blind also?" Jesus said to them, "If you were blind, you would have no sin; but now you say, 'We see.' Therefore your sin remains.*

There was no repentance in the Pharisees; this *decision killed* their chance to see the light. Because of this, the darkness didn't lighten up, it tightened up and solidified their citizenship in the kingdom of darkness. Those who *think they have it all together* are in darkness. One of the most *dangerous* things for a Christian; is to believe they have arrived - this is *pride. Prideful* men and women have *a knack for missing a truth* while staring at it head on. *Prideful* men and women love to use Scripture on others. But they never examine themselves by the Scriptures. So when you try to explain a Scripture to a prideful person, their response is usually, *"yeah but..."* then they continue to *justify* whatever it is they are trying to justify, whether it is their behavior or their belief. In this attitude, so-called philosophies are generally born and the person will experience blindness in the simplest of Scriptures; as we have seen here.

In the Book of Romans, we find when a person *rejects* the truth of God's Word, or *exchanges* the truth of God's Word for *a lie,* the person *opens the door* for all the works of darkness such as: *a debased mind, homosexuality, filled with all unrighteousness, sexual immorality, wickedness, covetousness or greed, maliciousness or malice, strife, deceit, evil-mindedness, backbiters, haters of God, violent, proud, boasters, inventors of evil things, disobedient to parents, undiscerning, untrustworthy, unloving, unforgiving* and *unmerciful.*

As mentioned before, *2ⁿᵈ Thessalonians 2:9-12* acquaints to us when we don't have a love for the truth, God will send these persons a *strong delusion* to believe the lie.

> Colossians 2:8
> *Beware lest anyone cheat you through philosophy and empty deceit, according to the tradition of men, according to the basic principles of the world, and not according to Christ.*

The word *'cheat'* in the above passage of Scripture refers to being plundered or being held as captive. In reference to the subject matter, the Holy Ghost is saying; *do not let anyone disqualify your walk with Christ with cheap and meaningless words.* An example of this is a man who is always promising to do something but is never able to keep his promises. This man is blind to his own inabilities. A philosophy is the love and pursuit of wisdom by *intellectual means* and moral self-discipline. *Philosophies* come from the minds of *carnal men*, not from God, and as *the Bible teaches us* in the books of Colossians and Corinthians, it is not *philosophy*, it is *trusting* in Christ alone for salvation. It is only then a person is able to shake off the blindness and all other constitutions of darkness.

The *Pharisees* were a group of men with a *self-conjured philosophy* on serving the Lord. The truth of God had been stymied in Jerusalem for years and the philosophy of religion became the so-called truth in the hearts of most religious leaders.

There was *no repentance* when the Pharisees heard the truth in the Words of Jesus. Their hearing had grown *dull* because they *didn't recognize* Jesus from the Scriptures. The darkness had them in its powerful *grip*.

> John 5:39
> *You search the scriptures, for in them you think you have eternal life; and these are they which testify of Me.*

These men *thought* they had their act together, but *blindness* had *disabled* them and they did not know it, so therefore they *could not see* the truth. The *praises of men* in the streets of Jerusalem elevated them into a *sense of arrival* and came to believe they had God all figured out. Their *high opinion* of themselves established the darkness within themselves and kept them from revelation knowledge or illumination in the person of Christ Jesus. When a person thinks he has God figured out – *they are blind* and *do not have a clue* they are lost and in need of a savior. The Savior was standing in front of them and they *did not recognize* Him. They read in the Scriptures He would *heal, deliver* and *show the way* to God – they saw these miracles happen in their sight but *they didn't recognize* Him. They couldn't put two and two together and when they tried, they came up with twelve.. For instance they *could not relate* the miracles, such have never been done before with the prophecies of the Messiah; Who would do miracles such had never been done. The darkness had them fully enveloped and *they couldn't see the truth* was standing in front of them.

Today, there are utterly millions of people who are in the *same condition* as these religious sects were in the days when Jesus walked the earth as a man. They are *cheated* through *philosophies, traditions of men* and just *plain ol' stubbornness* and *will not accept* Jesus at His Word.

When we *do not accept* the Word of Christ Jesus as truth and *neglect* to be a doer of the Word, then we will find ourselves in darkness.

Notes:

Chapter 8

Rebellion

Another work of darkness is *rebellion*. Rebellion is an open armed and organized resistance to a constituted government. Rebellion is a show of *defiance* toward an authority or established covenant; here, the authority is God.

> *Isaiah 14:12-14*
> *How you are fallen from heaven, O Lucifer, son of the morning! How you are cut down to the ground, you who weaken the nations! For you said in your heart: 'I will ascend into heaven, I will exalt my throne above the stars of God; I will also sit on the mount of the congregation on the farthest sides of the north; I will ascend above the heights of the clouds, I will be like the Most High.'*

The very first *act* of rebellion was *committed* by an angel named Lucifer. He is the *author* of rebellion and the father of lies. The Gospel of John calls him a *murderer* from the beginning and he has many titles or descriptions. He is called Abaddon in *Revelation 9:11*, the Accuser of the brothers in *Revelation 12:10*, the Adversary in *1 Peter 5:8*, The Angel of the Bottomless Pit in *Revelation 9:11*, and Apollyon which is also in *9:11*. He is also called Beelzebub in *Matthew 12:24*, Belial in *2 Corinthians 6:15*, The God of this world in *2 Corinthians 4:4*, a Murderer in *John 8:44*, and the Old Serpent *Revelation 20:2*. He is the Prince of Demons in *Matthew 12:24*, and the Prince of the Power of the Air in *Ephesians 2:2*. He is the Prince of Darkness in *Ephesians 6:12* and the Wicked One in *Matthew 13:19*. This dark angel is very *powerful* and has been on the job a very long time. He opposes God and he is the leader of the *open, armed,* and *organized*

43

resistance against the One Who sits on the throne, the True and Living God. His rebellion has been an open defiance toward God's established authority and covenant before the beginning of time.

Notice in Isaiah that Lucifer didn't speak his rebellion with his mouth, God discerned his *thoughts* and they were enough to bring judgment on the son of the morning. *"For you said in your heart."* When light is shed on darkness it will *expose* the *intents* of the heart and Satan's thoughts *exposed* him for what he was. Satan is the king of darkness and one of the things he *desires*, is to undo God's work.

In the Gospel of Jesus according to *Mark 4:15*, the parable of the sower is a great explanation of spiritual truths. When we sit back and watch, we see this parable unfold almost every day. Everyone on the face of the earth will fulfill a Scripture. Some will fulfill the Scripture, *"Well done thy good and faithful servant,"* while others will fulfill *"get away from me you workers of iniquity."* We all will fulfill one or the other; it is up to us to decide which one.

"Behold, a sower went out to sow, and as he sowed, some seed fell by the wayside; and birds came and devoured them.

Some people will not understand the Gospel at all and will *lose* the free gift of salvation almost immediately. Why? Because these people do not care much for the Gospel and they have strongholds that are so powerful; they *won't be able to see* the light of salvation.

After a person has heard the Word of God, Satan, or the birds in reference to this text, will come with *doubt* and *unbelief.* He will suggest to the person that heard the Word of the Lord, "That it's not true," or "that's the white folk's religion," or "that's black folk's religion." Or they will try to play it off with, "they are a bunch of hypocrites or fanatics," Sometimes he will try to *influence* you through the *prejudices* of the day. "You should never listen to a white or black or a woman pastor." This is *rebellion*. Satan knows you, he has been watching you all of your life, and you have been in his army *rebelling* against God all of your life and you probably made him a good hand. The only power he really has is *the power of suggestion*. He will use comments

44

of *narrow-mindedness, chauvinism, bigotry, intolerance, bias,* and *hatred* to keep your *mind programmed* to the ways of darkness and keep you in *rebellion*. So if you decide to change your lifestyle and come to the Lord Jesus Christ, he will try to play on your *old nature* to keep you from obtaining your new nature.

Sometimes he will *whisper* words of rebellion to your spirit that God does not exist. If there is a God, then why are babies dying. Why are good people dying at an early age? If there is a God, why is the world so messed up? If there is a God, why doesn't he heal your momma, daddy or sibling? If there is a God why is there so much disease in the world today? Where was God in the tornado that killed those people, and on and on? The devil is good at *creating doubt* and *unbelief*; he has a lot of experience but he has *no power*. All he can do is *suggest* or try to plant a *thought* in your mind. When you go for it, then you are in for the ride of your life.

Sometimes Satan will heap *condemnation* on the person's past sins. If a person was a thief, he would remind the person of their thievery. If the person was caught up in sexual immorality he would run the video in the person's mind all of the exploits the person had been involved in. He may even say, you have done some things even God will not forgive. In any event, the Word is stolen from the heart of the person who has just heard the Word. If he could get in with that *suggestion*, then he will just give you the bat so that you can go to the closest corner and *beat yourself up*. In the end, you rebelled against God.

> John 10:10
> "*The thief does not come except to steal, and to kill, and to destroy. I have come that they may have life, and that they may have it more abundantly.*"

The first person in the parable did not understand the Word that was sown. Maybe, he didn't care much for the Gospel of Christ. Throughout the history of mankind, what is not understood is usually killed. The seed that would have changed his life from the kingdom of darkness to the kingdom of God is stolen and eternal life is lost.

Some fell on stony places, where they did not have much earth; and they immediately sprang up because they had no depth of earth. But when the sun was up they were scorched, and because they had no root they withered away.

and

But he who received the seed on stony places, this is he who hears the word and immediately receives it with joy; yet he has no root in himself, but endures only for a while. For when tribulation or persecution arises because of the word, immediately he stumbles.

Some will hear the news of salvation and will receive it with joy. They are so excited they *tell* their friends and every one they can think of about the *good news* of Christ in their lives. Some of the people will be happy one has made the *decision* to leave the darkness to become a child of God, in the covenant of God. However, all friends are not as happy as the newly saved person. Some friends will think or even say, "It won't last. I'll give it a week or a month and he will be in sinning daily with the rest of us."

I have seen brothers who have given their lives to the Lord, jump around in the church with raised hands worshipping the Lord. They start repenting of things they did years ago. They tell everybody they see about their conversion. And I have seen these same brothers six months later, fall back into the saddle of darkness. How does this happen? When a person gets saved, they must *root* themselves in the Word of God. We must build ourselves up on the foundation of the truth of Jesus by *reading* the Bible every day. *Faith comes by hearing and hearing by the Word of God.* We must *commune* with the Lord daily. But most importantly, we must *abide* in the Word we have learned. When we *abide*, (or *live* the Word), in what we have learned from the Lord, God will raise us up to another level in *understanding* and *revelation*. This process will repeat even after we become *mature* in the Lord. But if we don't, we will find ourselves fulfilling the second seed in this parable.

As mentioned before, some people will even try to *lure* you back into the *bondage* in which you were delivered. For instance, if you were a marijuana smoker before you were saved, your old dope smoking buddies will try to *seduce* you into smoking weed with them, or if you were a heavy drinker they would *entice* you with alcohol. It is the same with *adultery, sexual immorality, gossiping, lying, stealing,* and the whole laundry list of sins that the person was caught up in. There are some people, male and female, whose entire mission in life is to cause a Christian to *stumble* and if possible *deny* Jesus as the Son of God, the Christ. If you deny Jesus, you deny God. So just like a dog, they return to the muck, *mire* and vomit they came out of.

Many times *tribulation* and *persecution* starts with a little name-calling like, "You're a fanatic, a Jesus Freak, or a Bible thumper." These people just want to *pressure* you to come back to a sinful lifestyle because they are lonely without you; after all you were the life of the party. *Peer pressure* plays a large part in tribulation and persecution because not everyone wants to follow God. This is especially true with gang bangers or cults. Most join a gang/cult for attention or just wanting to belong to something or a cause. When a gangbanger/cult member attempts to quit becoming a Christian, he /she are met with tremendous *opposition, hostility, disapproval,* and *conflict.* Before long, and as the pressure mounts, the newly saved person will start backing away from the Word that was sown in their heart. They will listen to the *false* devotion ideas, and plans of homies, friends, or loved ones instead of listening to the problem solver and they will eventually *fall off* and return to the former way of life. Pressure can bust pipes and make water run uphill, and when the person *adhere* to peer pressure, they will *submit* to it and go *back* to darkness from whence they came. So in the end, you rebelled against God.

And some fell among thorns, and the thorns sprang up and choked them.

and

Now he who received seed among the thorns is he who hears

the word, and the cares of this world and the deceitfulness of riches choke the word, and he becomes unfruitful.

The third person who heard the Word also receives it with joy. However, the person is so *caught up* in the world and on material things; the Word of God is *choked out* of his life. The *cares* of paying rent or making car payments, insurance, groceries, husbands/wives, sports, hobbies, gossip television, and children, begin to take top priority. I am not saying that once you become a Christian, you start ignoring your husband/wife and kids and other responsibilities, I am saying it is imperative, or absolutely necessary God has *priority* in your life, and as you do this, God will take care of you and yours. God spoke to me once and said, *"When you take care of my business, I will take care of your business."*

Matthew 6:33
Seek first the Kingdom of God and His righteousness and all these (houses, food, paying bills, clothes) things will be added to you.

Trying to obtain large amounts of money, gaining wealth, is one of the most *dangerous* things a person can get caught up in. There have been many who have *compromised* godly ethics to gain wealth and fame. This person's mind will constantly *think* of ways of obtaining money instead of ways of pleasing God. He will be so consumed with building up his domain the Word of God just slowly fades out of his or her life.

Jesus teaches us in *Matthew 6: 26-33*, that God knows all things. He knows when a single sparrow falls to the ground. So we should not worry about eating, drinking, the clothes we wear or the house we live in. The person in this part of the parable does not seek the Kingdom of God for very long but he lets the cares of life *control* his *thoughts* and *actions*. Christians should not be controlled by the *cares* of life; Christians should allow the Holy Ghost lead them by the Word of God.

But others fell on good ground and yielded a crop; some a hundredfold, some sixty, some thirty. He who has ears to hear let him hear!"

The fourth person is so happy he's saved - nothing else matters but the Word of God. This is the person whom, when the new wears out, the person still has the *zeal* to seek God's face instead of His hand. This person is *trying* to please God in everything he does and he *acts* out the commission God has given to every man. This person *pushes* peer pressure to the side and *continues* in the covenant God called him/her to. This person does not let the cares of the world bother him/her but *trust* God is faithful and will protect him/her and take care of him/her as they go through life. As we take care of God's business, God will take care of our business. This is the person who is led by the Holy Spirit and *renews* their mind every day by reading Matthew, Mark, Luke and John and the epistles which were written to him, the church.

The Old Testament is great for history and shows numerous examples of God's relationship with His children. The Old Testament gives us loads of information on God's character and examples of His grace. The Old Testament prophets warn us and give us examples on the love and judgment of God. The Old Testament is the "Book of What Happened." It is a *foreshadow*, or a *prophetic* Word of things to come. For the *prophesies* of the Old Testament has become truth *revealed* or evident for all to see in the New Testament. On the other hand, the epistles are instructions written to us, the Church, for today's living up to the last days and the return of Christ.

The fourth person in the parable is one who *communes* with God every day, and *thinks* on the goodness of God in the heat of the day and in the still of the night. This is the person who *walks* in; the love of God, in the power of God and in the wisdom of God. This is the person who is blessed in everything he does, and the power of God makes this person mighty in word and deed. This person has forsaken the darkness and walks in the light.

Therefore hear the parable of the sower: When anyone hears the word of the kingdom, and does not understand it, then the wicked one comes and snatches away what was sown in his heart. This is he who received seed by the wayside. But he who received the seed on stony places, this is he who hears the word and immediately receives it with joy; yet he has no root in himself, but endures only for a while. For when tribulation or persecution arises because of the word, immediately he stumbles. Now he who received seed among the thorns is he who hears the word, and the cares of this world and the deceitfulness of riches choke the word, and he becomes unfruitful. But he who receives seed on the good ground is he who hears the word and understands it, which indeed bears fruit and produces: some a hundredfold, some sixty, some thirty."

This parable is about salvation and being transferred into the Kingdom of God. Everyone will hear the Word of God but it affects people in different ways.

The secret of successful living in the Kingdom of God/Heaven is *letting Jesus live* His life *through you*. When you sow the Word of God into the lives of the people the Holy Spirit sends you to, you are responsible for the power of the Word changing their lives. When we speak what the Holy Ghost tells us to speak then, lost souls are added to the Kingdom of God. God depends on His children to add to His family. *"Do business till I come…"* Just as you *heard* the Word and *received* it with joy, you must do the same for others. So when you *yield* to Him and *allow* Him to *operate through you*, you will be operating in His Kingdom. The Kingdom of God - The Kingdom of Light.

Chapter 9

Rebellion continued

There are many, many people who are living in *rebellion* today. In this chapter we will look at how we commit rebellion against the Lord.

> Hebrews 3:8
> *Do not harden your hearts as in the rebellion, in the day of trial in the wilderness.*

In the last chapter we talked about rebellion as an *open, armed* and *organized resistance* to a constituted government. Rebellion is a show of *defiance* toward an authority or established covenant.

God tells us the Nation of Israel rebelled against Him. How did the nation rebel against God? We will have to look into the Scriptures for God's examples of rebellion. But first a quick look at the history of Israel.

God chose a man named Abram to be the Father of Faith. He chose him to build a nation through him so He could show the world His sovereignty, His rule, His power, His authority, His autonomy, and His dominance throughout the earth.

> Genesis 12:1-3
> *Get out of your country, from your family and from your father's house, to a land that I will show you. I will make you a great nation; I will bless you and make your name great; and you shall be a blessing. I will bless those who bless you, and I will curse those who curse you; and in you all the families on the earth shall be blessed.*

God did many mighty works through Abram, and he stayed *faithful* to God in all times. God made him *victorious* in every conflict that accosted or confronted him. Everywhere Abram went, he *represented* God righteously. God told him he and his wife would have a son when he was seventy-five years old. It took twenty-five years for his son to be born, through the years he did not waver at the promise of God through unbelief; but was *strengthened* in *faith*, giving glory to God and being *convinced* or *fully persuaded* what God had promised, He was also able to perform. Did he make some mistakes along the way? Yes he did, but the bottom line is he remained faithful to God. Abram *believed* God and God accounted it to him as *righteousness.*

God told Abraham his descendants, the nation of Israel, would be in bondage for 430 years, to the day. God's Word came to pass because Israel was in slavery to the powerful Egyptian nation for that length of time. God's sovereignty is unmatched. During these four-hundred and thirty years I believe the pride of Egypt was running very high. They thought they were invincible and they had God's chosen people in bondage.

Now Egypt worshipped many false gods and they also worshipped the Pharaoh as god. These *false gods hated* the True and Living God and *they knew* the promise God had made to Abram. *They did not want* the nations of the earth to be blessed so *they used* the nation of Egypt to oppress the children of Israel.

Egypt was the most powerful nation on the planet at that time. Their king, Pharaoh, was considered a god and was worshipped as god and king. However, we know God is a jealous God, (See *Deut. 5:7-9*) and His children were under the rule of Pharaoh, a false god. God's wrath was not necessarily against the Egyptians alone but the gods of the Egyptians, *(See Ex. 12:12).*

The Egyptians went to war many times and they conquered many nations. They *depended* on their gods to save them and to project them into their many victories. In essence it was false gods against false gods. They were rather *confident* in their abilities and their god's abilities to protect them from of all enemies of their state. So when Moses came to

Pharaoh and demanded them to let the children of Israel go, they would not, because they had confidence in their armies and in their gods.

But through the plagues of water turning into blood, frogs, lice, flies, diseased livestock, boils, hail mixed with fire, locust, darkness, and death upon the first born, God put to naught Egypt's gods and the people who worshipped them. God attacked each god of Egypt with a specific plague. God filled the sky with darkness on Ra, the sun god. God turned the Nile River to blood because the Egyptians worshipped the god of the Nile. God destroyed the image of power on the god of vegetation and so on. Israel only saw the destruction of the wicked who worshipped other gods. They finally let the people go.

When Israel left Egypt, they left with all their *spoils*. They took all their *gold*, all of their *silver*, their *clothing; everything* that had *value*, Israel took. They journeyed for a while and God told them to rest by the Red Sea.

Exodus 14:3-4
For Pharaoh will say of the children of Israel, 'they are be-wildered by the land; the wilderness has closed them in' Then I will harden Pharaoh's heart, so that he will pursue them; and I will gain honor over Pharaoh and over his army, that the Egyp-tians may know that I am the Lord. And they did so.

After the children of Israel left, Pharaoh and the people wondered why they had et them go. So they packed up their 600 choice chari-ots, with captains on every one of them, and the army and *pursued* Israel. When Pharaoh's army *found* the children of Israel backed to the Red Sea, the people *panicked*.

They said to Moses, "Because there were no graves in Egypt, have you taken us away to die in the wilderness? Why have you so dealt with us, to bring us up out of Egypt? Is this not the word that we told to you in Egypt, saying, 'Let us alone that we may serve the Egyptians'? For it would have been better for us to serve the Egyptians than that we should die in the wilderness."

The *seed* of rebellion was *growing* in the hearts of some of the Israelites. They *looked* at their present circumstances and *lashed out* at Moses. However, they were not really lashing out at Moses and Aaron, they were lashing out at God. It is amazing how quick we forget what God has delivered us from. Some of us were drug addicts, some of us were thieves and liars, some of us were back biters and gossips, some of us were sexually immoral, some of us were whoremongers, and some of us were murderers. Whatever it is we came from, we cannot forget Who delivered us. *Doubt* and *unbelief* is an absolute *killer to faith*. When they *complained* against Moses, they complained against the Lord.

This is really an astonishing statement. They, as a people, had been praying for deliverance from the Egyptians for 400 years. There were many nights when they *complained* about their bondages and what they would do *if* they ever got out of their *current* situation. They *watched* with disdain as the slave masters beat them, killed others, and fed them poorly. They were talked down to and greatly disrespected as human beings. They wanted out! The entire nation *saw* the plagues on the Egyptians, but most importantly they witnessed the fact; they were not affected by any of the ten plagues. They got a glimpse of *Psalms 91:8 - "Only with your eyes you shall see the reward, destruction of the wicked."* We can see the signature of darkness in this situation. Darkness has a way of making a person forget the good things in the past and *focus on*, what they deemed as disaster, in the present. God calls this rebellion. Why? Because the children of Israel *didn't believe* in God as a deliverer even when He has already shown them He is The Deliverer. In *Matthew 8:26*, Jesus calls it, *"Ye of little faith."*

> *Exodus 12:12*
> *Is this not the word that we told you in Egypt, saying, "Let us alone that we may serve the Egyptians"? For it would have been better for us to serve the Egyptians than that we should die in the wilderness."*

This would have been a blow to God if He hadn't known their condition – they said they would rather serve the Egyptians in bondage than to serve the True and Living God in freedom. God certainly verified His mercy with the *ignorance* of His children by not destroying them.

In the 14th chapter of Exodus, we see God had a plan which re-iterates, *"My thoughts are higher than your thoughts and My ways are higher than your ways."* God's plan was to demonstrate to the Egyptians; He alone was God, and there is no other god who can compare to Him, *(v. 4)*. The children did not understand God's plan because of *ignorance*, and as we have discussed before, *ignorance is a trait of darkness.* They did not have any spiritual *awareness* or spiritual *understanding* as the men in *John 15:15.* So they rebelled.

God told Moses to camp by the Red Sea, then He put *hooks* in the mouths of Pharaoh and the Egyptian army and caused them to come out against His people. He *urged* Pharaoh to bring out his 600 choice chariots with captains over each chariot to pursue the children of Israel. Israel saw the destruction of Pharaoh and his army, they witnessed the once powerful nation drown in the Red Sea. They gave God praise but they did not continue in praise.

A *dangerous* trait of darkness is getting *comfortable in the condition* that you are *in*. Even though they said they wanted deliverance, it was just talk. Some of the children were *comfortable* with the harsh taskmasters of Egypt. They had *grown accustomed* to the conditions of slavery. In slavery, every day was *the same*, there were no surprises – it was dreary day after dreary day. Even though they were treated badly, they had a roof over their heads and food on the table. They were able to marry and have children. Even in slavery, they *had some stability* in their lives; they didn't live by faith because their lives were *accustomed* by *their senses.* The Egyptians met their basic needs.

It is a *dangerous* thing when today's Christians gets into a *comfortable* cycle as the Children of God did in Exodus 12. There are far too many brothers and sisters in Christ sitting on the bench in church buildings who are too *satisfied* to allow the Holy Spirit to work through them. As long as the rent is paid, food in the refrigerator, air-conditioning in the summer, heat in the winter, and the satellite TV is baby-sitting little Johnny or Shaniqua, life is considered - good.

In this condition, *the people call* themselves blessed.

When a person's hunger for the Lord diminishes, the revealed Word of God will also *diminish* in the person. The vision of God also *dwindles* because the *comfort* of the *flesh* has chased the Holy Ghost away. In order to have a vision of God, you must be full of God, via the Holy Spirit, (or you soon will be). When a person gets comfortable, then God is *not* absolutely necessary in day to day life. This by itself is a *form of rebellion*. This path leads the person back into the darkness from which they came.

Another word for *darkness* is the Greek word '*Scotia*' and it is presented in *John 12:46*.

Scotia in this passage of Scripture is defined as: gloom, evil, sin, obscurity, night, ignorance, and moral depravity. The New Testament uses this term in a metaphorical sense of *ignorance of divine truth,* man's sinful nature, total absence of light, and *a lack or spiritual perception*.

No one in their right mind would want to live in an atmosphere of *gloom, evil, sin, ignorance* and *moral depravity*. Yet millions of people live in this state and they cannot understand why. They do not know when they reject the Word of God, they reject knowledge and understanding. *Ignorance* is defined as: Lack of knowledge or education. It is also defined as unawareness of something, often of something important. God says – *"My people are destroyed for lack of knowledge"*. *Hosea 4:6*. Scotia is spiritual darkness and basically describes everything *earthly* or *demonic* that is at *enmity* with God.

Scotia is *the system* of the evil one. Satan projects *gloom, doom* and the *unworthiness* to everyone alive. Satan *hates* God so much, the only way he can get back at God is by *corrupting* His children, His prized possessions; the human race that was originally created in His image.

Since the *fall* of Adam and Eve, the entire human race is born with a hook of darkness in his or her jaw. This hook is a *stronghold* which holds men and women in the nature of *sin* and *darkness*. When people desire to be good, the hook of darkness keeps them *bound* without a natural way of escape. Jesus came to give each person on the planet a chance to come out of the *gloom, evil, sin, obscurity, ignorance* and *moral depravity*. The hook is what *keeps us* in darkness but

Jesus came and destroyed that hook that held us bound.

> *1 John 3b*
> *For this purpose the Son of God was manifested, that He might destroy the works of the devil.*

When a person receives this *revelation*, 'Jesus Christ has destroyed the works of Satan', then he will truly become *free*. What does this mean? It means we are no longer ignorant of the ways of darkness. We are able to *recognize* it for what it is and respond accordingly. *"It is written"*

> *John 8:31*
> *Then Jesus said to those Jews who believed Him; "If you abide in My word, you are my disciples indeed. And you shall know the truth, and the truth shall set you free."*

When we *abide* in the Word, the truth will become our nature. *Abide* means to stay in a given place, state, relation, or expectancy. It means to continue, dwell, endure, be present and remain. Jesus is saying when we *live* in His Word; when we continue to live by His Word, when we are *present* and *remain* on what He taught and what He preached, we would *know the truth* and it is the truth of Jesus that *makes* us free. We would not be ignorant but *knowledgeable* according to the *wisdom* of God leading us in our lives.

Jesus never promised us a bed of roses while we are on this earth, but when we endure the hardship that sometimes comes in our lives, the truth of who we are and Whose we are will carry us through anything the devil throws at us. When we *know* the truth and *live* the truth, we are truly *free* from the ways of the kingdom of darkness.

> *Matthew 7:24-25*
> *Therefore whoever hears these sayings of Mine, and does them, I will liken him to a wise man who built his house on a rock: and the winds blew and beat on that house; and it did not*

fall for it was founded on the rock.

Whoever listens to the teachings of Jesus is smart. Whoever listens to the teachings of Jesus is a survivor. Why? Because He is life and when we live in His Word, we have life. We have protection because we are no longer ignorant, and have a way of escape. We are not to be hearers only, but we are to actually do what the Master says. We are to live as the Master has called us to live. This is the difference between *hearing* and *doing*. When a person is doing what he/she heard the Master tells us, then we are living in the light.

> *Matthew 7:26-27*
> *But everyone who hears these sayings of Mine, and does not do them, he will be like a foolish man who built his house on sand: and the winds blew and beat on that house; and it fell. And great was its fall.*

Both of the houses were beautiful. But it is not the beauty of the house that makes a house *stand*. It is the good and solid foundation which makes the house sturdy. *Our house*, or our physically bodies may be adorned with fine cloths and jewelry, but if our *belief system* is not in Christ, then we will *fall*. Our *foundation* is the Word of God and as we feed on the Word of God daily, our foundation gets stronger and stronger. So when the trials of life accost our lives, we can withstand the storm and be more than conquerors because of the strength of the Word within us. When we *pray* and *intercede* for others, when we *commune* with the Lord, when we are obedient to the lifestyle we are called to, when we give God priority in our lives and love others as we love ourselves then we are working the covenant He laid out for us.

Storms will come on the righteous and the unrighteous. The difference is, in the middle of the storm, where is our *trust*. Because what we have been *studying*, how we have been *living*, and what we have been *saying*, will make all the difference in the outcome of our storm.

Storms could be troubles with our *finances*, or our *health*, or our *peace of mind*. Trouble can come in all different sizes, shapes, and from any direction. But when we live our lives based on the Word of our Lord and Savior, we will get through the storm and will come out of the storm stronger and wiser than we were before the storm.

Notes:

Chapter 10
Satan Wants to Make Men Turn Away From God

Job 2: 4-5
So Satan said to the Lord, Skin for skin! Yes, all that a man has
he will give for his life. But stretch out Your hand now, and touch
his bone and his flesh, and he will surely curse You to Your face.

The story of Job is one of the most interesting stories in the Bible.
This story reveals the nature of the enemy and how he tries at every
turn to *discredit* the One Who sits on the Throne. This story also
conveys God's protection and how He limits the devil's *interference*
in the lives of men.

Job's story starts with the good report of his *integrity* and *charac-*
ter. The Bible says he was an outstanding man, blameless, upright,
feared God and shunned evil. But to Satan, Job would be a trophy
if he could *cause* Job to curse God to His face. What a challenge!
When we think about it, we can almost see the snarly smile of the evil
one anticipating a fall of a man God was proud of.

Job 1:6-8
Now there was a day when the sons of God came to present
themselves before the Lord and Satan also came among them.
And the Lord said to Satan, "From where do you come?"
So Satan answered the Lord and said, from the going to and
fro on the earth, and from walking back and forth on it."
Then the Lord said to Satan, "Have you considered My ser-
vant Job, that there is none like him on the earth, a blameless
and upright man, one who fears God and shuns evil.

God did a little bragging on Job. He was letting Satan know, not everyone is living by the world's standard. God boasted on Job's lifestyle, that he is a person who lives *righteously* and has the utmost respect for Him. Not only does Job have the utmost respect for God, he also *eschews, disdains, avoids,* and *shuns* evil.

> *Job 1:9-10*
> *So Satan answered the Lord and said, "Does Job fear God for nothing? Have you not made a hedge around him, around his household, and around all that he has on every side? You have blessed the work of his hands, and his possessions have increased in the land.*

The witness of Job's testimony is really astounding. This verse indicates he had been trying to get at Job but the Lord's protection kept the devil from interfering with his life. *"Does Job fear God for nothing?"* It would be nice if the devil would have this testimony from every church member today.

This Scripture depicts God's protection for his people. God's protection is for those who walk *blameless, upright,* shuns, avoids, and rejects evil. It is for those who do not purposely *dabble* in sin and *play* in iniquities. It is true, we do fall in sin at times, but we get back up and ask God to forgive us and move on. When we do, God forgives us and throws our sins into the Sea of Forgetfulness. However, we do not use God's mercy and grace as a license to sin. Such comes from an *evil heart*, and God will not be played and He will not tolerate it. When we take the effort to *walk uprightly* from our heart, then God blesses us with His protection. We all go through problems and difficulties, but the beautiful thing is; we go through them. God's protection will not allow us to perish.

Job was the kind of man who trusted in the Lord and was a man of good works. He dwelt in the land and fed on the faithfulness of God, as *Psalms 37:3* declares. The Bible tells us *when we delight ourselves in the Lord, He will give us the desires of our hearts. Psalms 37:5.* The word *delight* means pliable, so we are *pliable* with the Lord, He gives us the desires of our hearts. To be *pliable* is to be *flexible* and to be *workable*. So when we trust in God; we also will have a hedge of protection around us and our household, our possessions will increase, and we shall have the desires of our hearts.

Job lived in the attitude of *Psalms 91*:

Psalms 91:1-2
He who abides in the secret place of the Most High shall abide under the shadow of the Almighty. I say of the Lord, "He is my refuge and my fortress; My God, in Him will I trust.

For those who *abide, live in* and *rely* on God, he shall have the protection of the Lord. God would be a *refuge, sanctuary, shelter,* or *haven* for all who trust in Him. When a man or woman of God takes this attitude, God says,

"Because you have made the Lord, who is my refuge, even the Most High, your dwelling place, no evil shall befall you, nor shall any plague come near your dwelling."

The *choice* is ours. We can either abide or not. If we do not abide in the *secret place*, then evil will befall us and we will be plagued with the activities of the kingdom of darkness. A lot of people want the protection of God but they do not want to abide under the shadow of the Almighty. They do not want to be *obedient* to the Word or walk in His ways. And there are some people who make an attempt to trust God, but they set a limit on how far to trust him. They may trust God for good health but not with their finances. God wants us to trust Him in every area of our lives, whether it is health, wealth, or even day to day *decisions* in our daily walk. When we do, we will be walking in the Kingdom of Light.

Job 2: 4-5
So Satan said to the Lord, Skin for skin! Yes, all that a man has he will give for his life. But stretch out Your hand now,

and touch his bone and his flesh, and he will surely curse You to Your face.

The Scripture shows Satan had to get permission to harm Job. God had bragged on Job and Satan's reply is, because You have him under Your divine protection, he is happy, rich and prosperous, in perfect health, and fears nothing. The devil goes on to say, if You took all he has, and cause sickness to come upon him, he will curse You (God) to Your face.

God responded, *"Behold, all that he has is in your power; only do not lay a hand on his person."* So the devil went out and influenced the Sabeans to rob Job of his donkeys, oxen and killed all but one servant. Then Satan imitated God as a consuming fire and burned up all of Job's sheep and the servants who were tending them with the exception of one servant. Then Satan swayed a band of Chadeans to raid Job of his camels and killed the tending servants also. Then in conclusion, Satan imitated God's rushing mighty wind and caused the house to collapse on all of Job's children.

In response to all the horrible news, Job arose, tore his robe, shaved his head, and fell on the ground to worship the Lord.

Job 1:21
He said, "Naked I came from my mother's womb and naked I will return there. The Lord gave and the Lord has taken away; blessed be the name of the Lord."

Satan wanted Job to turn away from God. He tried his best to cause Job to curse God but Job blessed the Lord. This attitude is a characteristic of living in the light. He had lost his home, his children, his livestock and most of his servants but he had the presence of mind to bless the Lord. Was he *hurting*? Yes! Was he *sad*? Yes! Was he *heartbroken*? Yes! Was he *aching*? Yes! Was he down? Yes! Yes! Yes! But Job *did not look* at the circumstances, he looked toward the Master, he looked toward the Lord, and worshipped Him. He *did not do* what Satan anticipated, Job *did not curse* God. He *did not sin* in this ordeal and God blessed him mightily.

Today, Satan still wreaks havoc in the lives of men. There is not a person on the planet who has not experienced heartache here or there. But most people do not realize it is Satan who comes to *steal, kill* and *destroy*. And when they do not realize the deed is *authored* by Satan, they *blame* God for it. There are numerous people who say it was an act of God Who took my baby away, or caused some personal disaster in their lives. Satan will *cause* these things to happen in the lives of men so they may blame God and *cause* them to *turn away* from God.

Notes:

Chapter 11
Satan Wants the Worship of Men

Exodus 20:1-5
I AM the Lord your God, who brought you out of the land of Egypt, out of the house of bondage. You shall have no other gods before Me. You shall not make for yourself a carved image- any likeness of anything that is in heaven above, or that is in the earth beneath, or that in the water under the earth; you shall not bow down to them nor serve them. For I, the Lord your God, am a jealous God, visiting the iniquity of the fathers upon the children to the third and fourth generation of those who hate Me.

The word *worship* in the Hebrew is *shâchâh*, (7812,) and is described as to depress, to prostrate in homage to royalty or God. It is to bow down, crouch, fall down (flat), humbly beseech, to (make) obeisance which is to genuflect, curtsy, bow or respect.

Jehovah says, I AM your God. He makes this personal and it was intended to ease the hearts of His children. He is attempting to put at rest any fears they may have had about Him because of His *awesomeness*, His *power* and His *might*. Yahweh told them I am the One Who brought you out of Egypt, out of the house of bondage. I am the One Who made a display of the Pharaoh and his entire army and caused the children of Israel to bear witnesses to that great event. Now He is telling them He is The God above all gods and they shall not serve any other god. He tells Israel they should not make any images in the likeness of anything anywhere to serve or worship. We are not to serve or worship *statues, figurines, pictures, representations, drawings* or *illustrations* of anything in the air (Sun. moon, stars or cancellations,), on

67

the earth, (men or animals), or in the seas (fish or mammals). God tells us not to worship the *things* He created for men since He is a jealous God and He will not play second fiddle to anyone or anything.

> *Deuteronomy 11: 16*
> *Take heed to yourselves, lest your heart be deceived, and you turn and serve other gods and worship them aside.*

God says, "take care, *watch* out, and be *alert*" because there are gods in the world who want your worship. He says, 'watch your heart' and don't let it *deceive* you or *convince* you to serve these other gods. God is saying when you prostrate yourselves in homage to other gods, when you bow down, crouch, fall down (flat), humbly beseech, to (make) obeisance which is to genuflect, curtsy, bow or respect these gods, His anger will be raised against you. He may not punish you at the point of time in worshipping these false gods, but it will certainly be held as *evidence* you do not belong to Him and *judgment* will be made against you on Judgment Day.

Another word for *worship* in the Hebrew is *câgad* and that also is to prostrate and worship. This word is found in the third chapter of Daniel when King Nebuchadnezzar built a sixty foot image of gold and gave a command, when the people hear the sound of the horn, flute, harp, lyre and psaltery, in symphony with all kinds of music, all shall fall down and worship the gold image; and whoever does not fall down and worship shall be cast into of a fiery furnace. So when the people heard these instruments, they worshipped according.

However, there were three young Israelites who did not *bow* and worship the image. When the Chaldeans saw the three Hebrew boys did not worship the image, they went and told King Nebuchadnezzar. They told the king the three Hebrew boys: Shad'rach, Mē'shach and Abed'-negō' did not bow down to the image nor did they *worship* the gods of the king. When the king heard these accusations, he called for the three Hebrew boys, Shad'rach, Mē'shach and Abed'-negō' and asked them if the indictments against them were true. Shad'rach, Mē'shach and Abed'-negō' told the king they would not serve his gods nor will they bow down to the image of gold.

Nebuchadnezzar tried to give them another chance to *change their mind* and said "when you hear the sound of the horn, flute, harp, lyre and psaltery, in symphony with all kinds of music, and will fall down and worship the gold image which I have made, good! But if you do not worship, you will be cast immediately into the midst of the burning fiery furnace.

The three Hebrew boys told him something of this nature; they did not need to *think* about it, *pray* about it or even *worry* about it. Then they said one of the most powerful *statements of faith* written in the Bible.

> *If that is the case, our God whom we serve is able to deliver us from the burning fiery furnace, and He will deliver us from your hand, O King. But if not, let it be known to you, O King, that we do not serve other gods, nor will we worship the gold image which you have set up.*

How is that for a faith statement? It didn't matter what the punishment was, Shad'rach, Mē'shach and Abed'-negō' *knew* their God and they also knew it would be better to be burned alive rather than to serve a *false god* or an *image* of gold made with the hands of men.

Nebuchadnezzar was a pawn in this epic story. Satan was *behind the scenes* filling Nebuchadnezzar's mind with *illusions* of grandeur, majesty, and opulence. Just as Satan wanted the praises of the elders, the four living creatures and angels of heaven, he wanted the praises of the people of the land. When Nebuchadnezzar was worshipped, so was Satan. It didn't matter if Nebuchadnezzar was receiving the *worship, adoration, bowing* and the *prostration* of the people, Satan was the real recipient of these praises because he wants and loves the worship of men.

Daniel 3:10-11
You, oh king, have made a decree that everyone who hears the sound of the horn, flute, harp, lyre and psaltery, in symphony with all kinds of music, shall fall down and worship the

gold image; and whoever does not fall down and worship shall be cast onto of a fiery furnace.

Both words *shâchâh* and *câgad* are defined as to fall down and prostrate oneself in worship to something. In this case, the worship is to a golden image which is a false god or an image of a false god.

Shad'rach, Mē'shach and Abed'-negō' did not worship the image of the golden effigy, and as promised, they were thrown into the fiery furnace which was heated seven times hotter than usual. When the guards opened the door, the flames of the fire from the furnace engulfed them. That should have been *a sign* for the king because his guards who made the preparations for Shad'rach, Mē'shach and Abed'-negō' to be burned to death, were overwhelmed by the intense heat and were burned up themselves.

When the king looked down into the furnace, he saw four men in the midst of the fire walking through and around the flames as if they were walking in the park and said, *"I thought they were only three men that we burned, but I see four and the fourth man looks like the Son of God."* When Shad'rach, Mē'shach and Abed'-negō' refused to worship the king even to the point of death, Jesus came down into the midst of the fire and walked with them. *I will never leave you nor forsake you.*

The word *"worship"* in Greek language has the same definition as the word for *worship* in Hebrew language: to prostrate oneself in homage (to reverence, to adore).

> *Luke 4:6-8*
> *And the devil said to Him, 'All this authority I will give to You, and their glory; for this has been delivered to me and I give it to whomever I wish. Therefore if You worship before me, all things will be Yours.*

The devil has a lot of gall. Here he is attempting to *persuade* Jesus, the son of God, the Creator of the Universe, and the sustainer of it, to bow before him to worship him. This teaches us if Satan has the audacity, the courageousness, the fearlessness and the boldness to try and *influence* Jesus to worship him, so he will certainly try to *entice, seduce, tempt,* and *lure* mankind into worshipping him in one way or another. As he attempted to do with Shad'rach, Me'shach and Abed'-nego', Jesus and others, he will try every Christian on the planet at one time or another.

The devil showed Jesus all the kingdoms in the world in a moment of time and promised them to our Lord and Savior if He would just bow down and worship him. Jesus replied, *"That you shall worship the Lord thy God, and Him only you shall serve."* Again, if he tried to convert Jesus to worship him, then he will try you. He may not try to influence us to bow down and worship him, but he will try to influence us to worship *material things* such as false religions, houses, money, children, movies, music, and clothing, whatever is at the forefront of the heart. It is not a sin to have these things, but when these things take *priority* over the Lord and His kingdom. Then you have a problem.

Satan loves worship. And one of his acts of rebellion against God is to secure men's worship to himself. Remember, in the subject matter here, rebellion is an open defiance or *warfare* against God. Many men and women throughout time have worshipped Satan through many of his cohorts, underlings, cronies, false pastors, false bishops, false prophets, false preachers and teachers, false worship leaders, carnal gospel artist, and others in one demonic form or another. He has a super *pride* issue and his *ego* is eternally gigantic. He craves the praise of people. He loves the *accolades of man* and he has secured the worship of men and women in many different names and in many different ways. Even though he loves the praises of man, he has absolutely no love for man, in fact - he hates us. But when he gets a *carnal* or a *natural* person that is willing to listen and ready for action, then he uses this person to spread the poison of his demonic doctrine through the *works of the flesh*. The *carnality* of a man's *mind* is the *gateway* to receiving the doctrine of demons and worship is one of his strongest desires.

The goal of Satan is to bring every man, woman and child to the same eternal death sentence which is the lake of fire and brimstone for eternal punishment along with him. Hell was not made for man but for the devil and the angels who rebelled against God. So every day, he tries to find a way to veer as many as he can off the path of righteousness in an attempt to spite God, the Creator of Man.

Exodus 20:2
I am the Lord your God, who brought you out of the land of Egypt, out of the house of bondage.

God is a good God and He brings us out of bondage. Satan wants us in *bondage* and the tools he uses is the *lust of the eyes*, the *lust of the flesh* and the *pride of life* to bring us and keep us in bondage if possible.

Exodus 20:3-5a
You shall have no other gods before Me. You shall not make for yourselves a carved image or any likeness of anything that is in heaven above, or that is in earth beneath, or that is in the water under the earth; you shall not bow down to them nor serve them. For I, the Lord your God, am a jealous God,

God is specific here; we shall have no other gods, period, point blank. He says He is a jealous God and He is giving us instructions on how to live a victorious life. God does not want us to be dogged about by the devil. God loves us and the instructions He gives us is for our own protection from ourselves and the devil. God knows Satan will try to seduce every person on the planet to worship him. So God tells us to worship Him and Him alone because He is The Only True and Living God.

Deuteronomy 18:10-12
There shall not be found among you anyone who makes his son or daughter pass through the fire, or one who practices witchcraft, or a soothsayer, or one who interprets omens, or a sorcerer, or one who conjures spells, or a medium, or a spiritists, or one who calls up the dead. For all, who do these things are an abomination to the Lord, and because of these abominations the Lord your God drives them out from before you.

In the history of countries, there have been various gods in which men worshiped and served. These nations did not have a covenant with God; Satan took advantage of this and influenced these nations to worship and serve him as God. Israel also fell victim to the devil's trappings and served false gods from time to time. Satan travels the earth to and fro, looking for someone, or a group of people he can influence to serve and worship him.

In *1 Kings 11:5* we find Satan as *Ashtoreth*, the Canaanite god that was worshipped as a *god of fertility*. They practiced sex as an avenue of worship and *astrology* as a doctrine or belief system, these gods was – and still are worshipped as the *goddesses* of love and war.

Rimmon is a Syrian god in the *Book of 2 Kings 5:18*. Rimmon is worshipped as the god of rain and thunder and was the local god of Damascus. So in order to get rain, the people had to worship this *entity* in order to appease this *resident demon* posing as God.

Adrannelech is another Syrian god found in *2 Kings 17:31*. This god required a little more than his demonic buddy, His demand of worship required children to be sacrificed by fire in order to be placated.

Bel, is the title for the Babylonian god *Merodach*, or *Marduk*, which is the *chief* Babylonian god. He is a fertility god found in *Jeremiah 51:44* and *Isaiah 46:1*. A fertility god is one who is in charge of the reproduction system of humans and agriculture. If these gods were not pacified through worship, the women were threatened with the possibility of barren wombs throughout the land. Another Babylonian god named Tammuz is found in *Ezekiel 8:14*. He is the deity in charge of vegetation. If the people did not praise and worship this false god, the people would not have crops and vegetables.

Egypt worshipped a myriad of demon gods, from Osiris the architect of the universe to the sun god Ra, to the god of the Nile and several hundred other gods. They had a god for every arena of life. Today, these Egyptian gods are one of the motivating forces in music today. They were also involved with calf worship.

Milcom and *Molech* are the gods of the Ammonites and are found in *1 Kings 11:4-8*. Their worship also included human sacrifices, especially children.

A god of the Moabites is *Chemosh* and is also found in *1 Kings 11:7*. The worship of Chemosh was equally as cruel as Milcom and Molech and is centered in astrology.

The Assyrians worshipped a god who was part man and part eagle named *Nisroch, 2 Kings 19:37*.

The story of *Dagon* is found in *1 Samuel 5:17*; he was the god the Philistines worshipped. He had the head, chest, and arms like a man, but the rest of his body was a fish. He was worshipped as the father of Baal.

Diana was a Greece's goddess of love and fertility, the virgin of hunting and child birth, *Acts 19:35*. Another god of Greece was *Jupiter, son of Zeus* who was worshipped as the creator of the universe. *Hermes, the son of Mercury,* was the spokesman for Zeus. All of these gods are of the same demonic system, but they have different names because they are operating in different countries that speak different languages. For instance, *Aphrodite* is a Greek god and *Venus* is a Roman god, the description of both these goddesses is *love, beauty* and *sexual desire*. They are both related to the fertility goddesses of the east named *Isis*. Satan takes the same game to different parts of the world to secure the worship of men and women. He knows if it will work in this country, it will work in other countries. After all, there are carnal men and all over the world who will fall for Satan's trickery.

Apollo, the Greek god and *Phoebus,* the Roman god are gods of prophecy, the patrons of music, and the healing arts. Their *symbol* is the sun bow or a lyre. They are part of the same *demonic system*, but have different names.

Athena, the Greek god and *Minerva* the Roman god are both goddess of war, wisdom, and the arts. They are of the same demonic system, but with different names according to their geographic location and language of the people.

The Greek god *Hephaestus* and the Roman god *Vulcan* are also one in the same. They are the gods of *trade, riches* and *good fortune*. They are reflected as the messengers of the gods and the patron *deities* of *thieves', tricksters,* and *con* men. They believe if they can trick you they can keep you in the spiritual atmosphere of darkness for as long as they want. They are the same demonic system, but have different names according to their geographic location and language of the people.

Zeus and *Jupiter* are the Greek and Roman gods who are close to the top of the demonic *chain of command*, according to the *myths*. They are considered as the kings of gods and men. They use the same demonic system, but different names.

Roman religion involved *cult* worship which was public and private. Roman families paid homage to *household spirits* while the state of Rome used colleges of official priest to make sure the actions of the families had the approval of their many gods. The approval of the Roman gods did not depend on the behavior of the person; however, it did depend on the *observance* and/or *participation* in religious *rituals*. Every Roman god had need of its own personal image or a statue built with bronze or stone. These *images* had temples and altars where the patrons could pay homage and respect in prayers and sacrifices to worship them. Open sex and orgies with family members and strangers were also a part of Roman worship.

Rome also worshipped their current Emperor (Caesar) of the times and like Pharaoh, they were considered as God. The demons that *manipulated* these countries are of the same demonic system, but different names.

One of the *customs* in Babylon compelled every woman to make a pilgrimage to the Temple of Aphrodite and have intercourse with a stranger once in her life. It didn't matter if they were rich or poor, small or great, each woman within the boundaries of Babylon was *forced*, duty-*bound*, and *obligated* to have sex with a stranger in the Temple of Aphrodite. The wealthy women who didn't want to mingle with the common women had an entourage that would deliver them to a private room within the temple; they would then do their *deed* and return home. Most of the attractive women did not have to wait too long to perform their once in a life-time task, but some of the comely women had to stand in line for three to four months before they are chosen, and *paid* to have intercourse with a total stranger.

Most of the common women sat with crowns of cords in their hair in the sacred area of Aphrodite; there were marked lines that ran through the crowd of women and the men would walk these lines and make their choice of which woman they would have sex with. The stranger would cast money in her lap and say, "*In the name of* Aphrodite (or the equivalent) the local god." It didn't matter how much money he gave her and the woman was unable to refuse because that would be a sin. She also could not reject anyone. Once the intercourse is completed, she was free to go home. Also, in Corinth, it is said that the temple of Aphrodite employed over a thousand temple *prostitutes* to serve the patrons as part of worship.

Today in India, when a poor family falls on hard times, the father of the family will dedicate his daughter to the local goddess as a temple prostitute. This way, the girl-child will have a profession that will help her family to survive. However, once a girl has been dedicated to the temple as a prostitute, she will never be able to marry.

All these gods are under the *rule* and *reign* of Satan. In each country these demons would entice the people to make a statue or some structure so they can worship them. They would also engage in illicit sex, for sex has a large format, or design in most false religions and cults.

Psalms 135:15
The idols of the nations are silver and gold, the works of men's hands. They have mouths, but they do not speak; Eyes they have, but they do not see; they have ears, but they do not hear. Nor is there any breath in their mouths. Those who make them are like them. So is everyone who trusts in them.

These idols of the nations, *the works of men's hands* are quite ridiculous. The people that worship these gods had to take care of these gods. They would have to wipe the dust off of these gods daily. If they needed to go somewhere, they would have to pack their gods, load them on their donkey before they can take them with them. If the idol fell to the ground and broke, they would have to repair their god so they may worship it. These gods were bought, sold, and some were stolen. So just think about this, these people *depressed* themselves; they *prostrated* themselves in homage to these man made gods. They *bowed down; fell down, kneeled* and *stooped* to these gods with the utmost respect and it did not occur to these people the gods they worshipped were being cared for by the worshipper. They were taking care of their god and did not realize they needed God to take care of them.

Throughout each and every generation, Satan and his *government of principalities, powers, rulers of the darkness of this world* and *wicked spirits in heavenly places* tries to influence the men of the earth to worship them as God. They are doing a very good job because there are thousands of religions outside of the truth of Jesus.

In the United States of America, Satan is worshipped in a superfluity of ways. Americans may not bow down to an effigy, carving, image, or a model, and most do not worship Satan directly. But homage is paid to him by our ways of life. He is worshipped as a god of *greed* where the *making, gathering* or *stealing* of money is the *focus* in life and is therefore an attitude of worship. Why? Because he doesn't depend on God to meet his needs, but instead depends on himself for self-sufficiency – thus he is a self-made man.

Satan is also worshipped in the music industry where most *lyrics promote* the lust of the flesh, lust of the eyes and the pride of life. He is worshipped in the film industry where examples of rebellion are *suggested, proposed, advocated* and even *advised* to rebel against God. There are movie makers who lie, misrepresent, pervert, slant, and garble God's character and truth in depicting Him on film for the use of entertainment. History is full of carnal men trying to produce a spiritual book/movie and substitute the wisdom of God for *sensationalism*, when in all actuality, they are producing and reinforcing a spirit of rebellion.

The media worships the beast by rehashing acts of *violence, greed, corruption*, and fueling the fire of *adversity* by the constant retelling of the shameful acts of carnal people. Many in media *induce* judgments through the *tone* of their voice, their posture and facial disdain (much like the Pharisees); they love the idea of God, but not His *ways*. The government worships the beast by not applying the counsel of God in the law.

In the Middle East, *territorial spirits* rule through religion, in third world countries the territorial spirits rule through drought and poverty, and then there are those who rule through *voodoo* and witch doctors. In America, demonic spirits rule through *sensual* and *fleshly* matters. Just about every area of commerce is geared toward *self-gratification*, it targets and appeals to our flesh, and our feelings. There are millions of people who live by their *feelings* and these people are *deceived* through their own sensual *mind-set*. They live off of what they *see*, what they *feel*, what they *taste*, what they *smell*, and what they *hear*. They take it as truth and live and die by it. Faith comes by hearing - false belief systems also come by hearing.

It is the nature of man to worship something. It doesn't matter where you go, you will find a nation, tribe, or tongue worshipping something or someone. Today, Satan is still the General of the kingdom of Darkness, and these demons are sent out to *disrupt* the flow of worship to God and try to *hi-jack* the worship of men for themselves. They are motivated to *kill* any move or progress in churches and ministries that are serving God in Spirit and in Truth. For the churches that are not serving God in Spirit and Truth, those who practice the leaven of the Pharisees, demons already have them in their employ. Then there are many satanic churches worshiping Satan loudly and proudly. They have their 'own bible' and they freely take on the characteristics of their father Satan. Then there are several other doctrines in the world today in open rebellion against the doctrine of Christ and will worship anything but God.

Another form of worship is; most of the world knows about Jesus but they don't serve Him or even listen to Him or read the Word of God. Instead, decisions are made to wax the car we worship on Sunday morning, or watch football and worship the players, baseball, soccer, basketball, or NASCAR all day. You see people prostrate theirselves to honor great athletes, they will stretch out their arms and move them in a bowing motion, giving homage to the sports player because of his greatness.

Some people would rather work many hours than spend them with God. And then we find some folks who would rather clean toilets than to worship the Lord. The prince of the power of the air has a world of *distractions* for the people of the earth. Many are worshipping him and do not realize it. Television, music, sports, making money, careers, drugs, lawn care, sex, sleep, recovery from Saturday night partying, self-gratification, are the *choices* people make instead of being in the presence of God, and then they will call themselves blessed. *Distractions* are keeping millions of people in bondage. *Priorities* are in disarray and out of order. This plays an important part in keeping people from the light of our Lord. There is nothing wrong with activities, but they should not replace God or our worship to God.

But for those who have given their lives to God to serve Him only, the princes of darkness will try to *steal* the joy of the saints, and will attempt to *destroy* all human beings through deceit, false doctrine, sickness, disease, and poverty, through desires and the characteristics of the human flesh. The tools these dark lords use are differences in people such as ideas, personality, gender, social status, race, nationalities, dialects, and religion.

These demons, like their spiritual father Satan, are *opposed* to all that is God. All demons and devils have a few things in common, they are all *jealous*. They are *envious* of the sons of God and their only desire in life is to *separate* the sons from the Father. They want to *bring us down* to their level. They are jealous for the worship and adoration of the people. These foul devils *operate* either through a spirit of *fear* or a spirit of *error*.

The evils that are practiced in worship to these gods are:

Immorality - When Israel was in Acadia Grove the people began to commit harlotry with the women of Moab. The children of Israel sacrificed and bowed down to their gods. God was angry with Israel, and told Moses to take all the leaders of the people and hang the offenders before the Lord, out in the sun. Then he told the judges to kill every one of the people that have joined themselves to Baal of Peor. *(See Num. 25:1-9)*

Divination – Some of the children of Israel and strangers who dwelt in the land were *sacrificing their children to Molech.* God pronounced judgment of death against all those who took part and those who knew about sacrificing their children to Molech, a demon god, and did nothing about it. *(See Lev. 20:1-6)*

Sacrilege – Belshazzar, the son of Nebuchadnezzar, hosted a feast where he brought out of storage the things that were taken from the Lord's temple. He and his lords, his wives and his concubines drank wine from the sacred vessels. They also praised the *gods of gold, silver, bronze, iron, wood* and *stone.* The party did not last very long because Darius the Meade navigated through the water tunnels of the castle and killed Belshazzar and took over the kingdom. *(See Dan. 5:4)*

Persecution - This is a most amazing story in the life of Elijah. He had killed 450 prophets of Baal, announced a three-year drought throughout the land and prayed for the three-year drought to end, he called fire on the captains of Ahab's army, and raise the dead son of the widow of Zarephath. But when the evil Queen Jezebel pronounced judgment on Elijah he fled. *(See 1 Kgs. 19:1-3)*

Prostitution – People have said that prostitution is one of the oldest professions in the world, but the children of Israel took it to a higher level. They had adopted some of the Canaanite rituals and practiced prostitution in the temple as a form of worship. Booths were even made for the women to practice their *craft.* Josiah had all these idols torn down and restored true worship to the Lord. *(See 2 Kgs. 23:7)*

Child sacrifice – God was angry with His children when they set up idols/abominations in the temple to *pollute* it. Not only that, *they build* high places/altars to burn their children in the fire in worship to these gods.

Chapter 12

Freemasons

The first thing we must understand is; *Freemasons is a religion* which accepts all religions as truth. Some pray to the Supreme Architect of the Universe, for most, it is the Egyptian god *Osiris* while others want worship from the citizens of the world. They are required to believe in a higher power, but they will not necessarily worship Jesus. They are *bound by an oath of secrecy* to the point that it is forbidden to testify against their brother in this organization/cult. They have also been working on the elimination of all distinction between the sexes. They are in high ranking areas in politics and finances in various countries; and are *obsessed* with the sun.

For years I believed our founding fathers were Christians, but I found out through study, George Washington, Ben Franklin, Thomas Payne and Thomas Jefferson and a host of others were Freemasons. They would mention God, for instance, 'One nation under God' but Jesus is not mentioned in most of their writings.

> *1 John 2:23*
> *Whoever denies the Son (Jesus) does not have the Father either; he who acknowledges the Son (Jesus) has the Father also.*
> (emphasis mine)

and

> *John 15:23*
> *He who hates Me, (Jesus) hates My Father also.* (emphasis mine)

Thomas Jefferson, the third President of the United States, and a

Freemason, had a wife, and another family, his extra-marital wife was Sally Hennings. This adulterous relationship produced several children with his slave woman and has been proven to be his children/descendants through the Thomas Jefferson bloodline by DNA testing.

President Jefferson wrote –
"But this syllabus is meant to place the character of Jesus in its true high light, as no imposter Himself, but a great reformer of the Hebrew code of religion, it is not to be understood that I am not with Him in all His doctrines. I am a Materialist; He (Jesus) takes the side of spiritualism; he preaches the efficacy of repentance towards forgiveness of sins; I require counterpoise of good works to redeem it."

Mark 8:38
For whoever is ashamed of Me and My words in this adulterous and sinful generation, of him the Son of Man will also will be ashamed when He comes in the glory of His Father with the holy angels.

President Jefferson said Jesus was just a great reformer of the Hebrew code of religion. He *did not see* Him as the Son of God; he *did not see* Jesus as a deliverer, a healer, as One Who would raise the dead. He *did not see* Jesus as his righteousness, or his salvation. He believed good works would save him.

Ephesians 2:8-9
For by grace you have been saved through faith, and that not of yourselves; it is the gift of God, not of works, lest anyone should boast.

There will be no boasting in what we did when we come to the Throne of God. We need to understand it is by grace we are saved. It is by God's unmerited favor that we are saved. It is by His great divine influence upon the hearts of men that leads us into His salvation. It is a gift, we cannot earn, we cannot buy it, and it is only by God's grace and what Jesus did at the cross to cleanse us from all our sins.

George Washington, also a Freemason, said,

"At the same time, I request you to be assured of my best wishes and earnest prayers for your happiness while you remain in this terrestrial mansion and that we may hereafter meet as brethren in the eternal temple of the Great Architect."

The California Freemasons says,

"No one owns God, just as surely as no one owns "truth." Not one among us can be truly certain about the nature of God, so the "Great Architect of the Universe" is a particularly apt reference to the Deity, as the reference acknowledges both the design and the designer without staking a claim on some exclusive jurisdiction. Deists, Christians - both Catholic and Protestant - Hindus, Muslims, Buddhists, and men of many other faiths have been welcomed into our Fraternity. One point of commonality is their belief in the one God. Masons believe there is one God and one God only. Masons also know that since time immemorial, people have employed many different ways of seeking and expressing what they know of God, of their experiences and relationship with that which transcends all knowing."

This data might sound honorable and substantial to the unlearned in Christ who are not acquainted or familiar with of the Word of God; but to the Christian who understands the clear teachings of the Bible, *Freemasonry is of the Devil. Freemasons recognize all gods as being one in the same,* which is also what New Agers teach. But the bottom line is that thought is a spawn from Satan.

Aleister Crowley, who nicknamed himself 666, said he had a vision from Horace the Falcon with the message to destroy Christianity. So this became his lifelong dream and work. His reason for living was to go against Christ.

It is said Crowley was the most demonic man who ever lived. He was an inspiration for the Church of Satan and he also inspired several popular groups from heavy metal to rock and roll bands. These bands have inspired hundreds, thousands and millions of people through the lyrics of their music. An example of this is the Beatles' song, *"Helter Skelter"* which was the inspiration for Charles Manson as he sent men and women on their killing spree. John Lennon wrote and sang a song, "My Sweet Lord," where the lyrics went from Hallelujah to *chanting* Dalai Lama and Krishna almost in the same breath. With the title, "My Sweet Lord" a person would think of Jesus – but John *mixed* eastern religions, or false gods, with the True and living God. You cannot mix the truth with the false – they cannot cohabitate.

There are several groups who would go to Tibet and voluntarily submit themselves to these eastern religions and get *brainwashed* on doctrine, *get high* on drugs, write music *under the influence* and go back to London or the United States with a string of hits. This story also relates to Robert Johnson who reportedly *sold his soul* to the devil for skills in playing the guitar. Today's world's system in the music industry involves *witchcraft, sorcery, drug use* and *homosexual acts*. It depends on who is involved. Fans would hear these lyrics over and over again accompanied of course with a catching rhythm and pounding hooks until it is *embedded in the soul* of men, women and children. Many people just love music and are unaware of the *spiritual repercussions* it leads to.

When the crowd roars and worships the artist with *applause* and *adoration*, it brings a smile to the devil because it is what he wants. When secular and even some gospel musicians are *praised, acclaimed, honored, applauded, celebrated* and *admired*, the element of *pride* has the ability to *swell* in the hearts of men. Secular artist do not have a defense for this, but gospel artist that abide in the Word will always *give* God the glory while secular artists *receive* the glory for themselves. When these artists raise their hands before the multitude of concert goers, their cries escalates and intensifies with praises and tears of admiration. Some roar their approval; some scream with envy, while others just pass out or faint. This is a form of worship and it parallels Satan's desires that are described in *Isaiah 14*, "*I will exalt my throne above the stars (angels) of God.*" The reason he wants to *exalt* his throne *above* God's throne is because he wants to be worshipped as God is worshipped. "*I will also sit on the mount of congregation, on the farthest side of the north.*" Satan wants to be lifted up and admired, but God cut him down. We can see the same characteristics with copious musicians and singers. They want to be lifted up, they want to be admired, longed for, adored, praised and worshipped as the best there is.

All music is not of the devil. All music does not promote lust of the eyes, lust of the flesh and the pride of life. There have been wonderful songs through the years that bring genuine joy to music lovers. There are sad songs, funny songs, and songs about relationships; there are songs that tell stories, songs for meditation, dance songs, and songs for line dancing. From blues to jazz, from pop to rhythm and blues, from classical to country, from blue grass to alternative to gospel, it all boils down to the *intent* of the writer and musicians.

I want to note; all singers and musicians are not pride hunters and seek the admiration of the multitude. There are great artist who just want to share the gift of music with others. These are the artist who gives thanks to God for *the talent God has blessed them with.* These artists are not to be confused with the ones who cuss, verbally violate women and men, advocate violence and lascivious living, and then thank God for their gifts. These artists are serving another god.

Crowley said, "Be strong o man! Lust, enjoy all things of sense and rapture: fear not that any God shall deny thee this."

The Influence of Music

Freemasons play an enormous part as a *power behind* the music industry today. They put millions of dollars into the industry to *promote* anti-God/Christ themes and the promotion of worship to other gods intentionally.

If you turn on the radio today to any top 40 station, you will hear lyrics like "I crash my car into a bridge and I don't care," or

"Allah and God are the same, so it is okay to be gay." And there are Heavy Metal songs that redundantly suggest that you kill yourself, kill your parents or other people. When Anita Ward recorded the song, "Ring my bell" just about every woman in the city was happily chirping the lyrics to that song. When R Kelly recorded "Your Body's calling for me," it inspired sexual encounters throughout the city. Then there are Madonna, Lady Gaga, Miley Cyrus and a host of others that use their sexuality to sell music

In the Hip Hop genre, Afrika Bambaataa says, "God gives us knowledge, which is infinite to even challenge if God exist or does not exist and to be rulers over the Earth, and for us to peek into space to the wonders of the universe. God gives you life, and He/She, gives you death. But we Amazulus cannot wait for God to appear and show His/Her, Whatever Self. When He/She/God is ready to show self, all the worlds in the universe shall see the force of who He/She/Whatever, is."

There are millions of children who listen to Afrika Bambaataa's music and children are easily influenced. The doctrine of Bambaataa is expressed through his music to the point of brainwashing the listeners to the ideals of his god/whatever.

KRS-One - the prophet of Hip Hop said, James Brown dying on Christ birthday shows not only he was Christ returned- but that hip hop has a chance, politically, to take a day. Let's celebrate James Brown! Hip hoppers *celebrate* the birth of their soul, the birth of Christ, the birth of their nature. Every Christmas we're gonna play James Brown records. All that white Jesus stuff is over! Matter of fact, 'I'm gonna call James Brown – James Brown the Christ! When you look at Jesus, look at James Brown."

Satan wants the worship of men and he does it through men in his *employ*. He does it through those who do not accept Jesus as the Christ, as the Son of the True and Living God, as our Redeemer and our Salvation. When we listen to music that thrives, beats and reverberates in our souls with its fruit of the flesh or with anti-Bible lyrics, it seeps down into our souls and we find ourselves singing and dancing to the *ideas, concepts, thoughts,* and *philosophies* of Satan.

Jay Z the rap star who calls himself *Hovah,* which is short for Jehovah, rapped the following tune, "Lucifer, Lucifer, son of the morning! Yes, this is a holy war; I wet y'all with holy water. Spray from Heckler and Koch automatic all the static, shall cease to exist like a sabbatical, I throw couple at you, take six! Spread love to all my thugs, I pour out a little Louis, to the head above – Yessir, and when I perish, the meek shall inherit the earth – til that time, it's on and poppin church." His wife, Beyoncé testified the demon *Sasha Fierce possesses* her when she performs on stage.

Some believe these lyrics are harmless, but the Bible teaches *life and death are in the power of the tongue and those who love it will eat its fruit - Psalms 18:21.* Whatever we are *saying* will *produce* either life or death. Most of the time, the *results* are not instantaneous, but at the end of the day you verbally *reap* what you verbally *sow.*

A lot of music today is anti-God! Why? Most music is *blasphemous* and promotes the evils of the flesh. Can you imagine a young boy or girl listening to this brand of music? Their young developing minds may not understand the lyrics but the song will be *imbedded* in their minds nonetheless. They will *repeat* the words in which they know nothing about until it becomes a part of their life. There are some, not all, rappers who scream and shout about their first amendment right to freedom of speech. But the only freedom they desire is to do the devil's work through music as a form of secular worship. These are some of the reasons for school shootings, shootings in the malls, movies and playgrounds. These are some of the reasons for murders, rapes, and every other form of evil. It's the influence of music and other media that has *the prince of the power of the air* wreaking havoc all around the world.

666 Mafia won an Academy Award for, "It's hard out here for a pimp" In the song 'Stay Fly' the background singers were melodically *chanting* in harmony, "Lucifer you are god and king." The devil desires the worship of men and these girls were giving it to him with thousands of people singing along. 666 Mafia goes on the say, "How can you have faith in a God that cannot even control creation? How can he lead you to salvation, there is no hope,

chaos only – welcome to the other side of reality, and this is your eternity." This is a sad quote coming from the mouths from sons of preachers of the Gospel.

Satan is *using* the 666 Mafia or 3Six Mafia mightily; he is receiving praise and *casting doubt* on the Word of God. Those who buy or download their music are also worshipping Satan and then adjust their lives to fit in with the doctrine of the group. All it takes is time and an open mind.

Finally 666 Mafia sang,

"beat, rob break murder, erase. Don't run, there is no escape. Bullets hit you right in the face – I'm not scared to catch a case. Sluz, hoes, blood on all yo clothes. Who will die next? Nobody knows. Insane mane-taking a drain bitc# I will empty your veins. I do not feel remorse – blow Mom off the porch. 45s, 9s, and the grenades. Blow yo girl off the stage. Mess with this super thug and get drugged-sweep yo body parts under a rug. Bury this butcher knife deep in yo guts – make you a nice warm blanket of mud – you fools ain't learned to see her burn – hollow points hit you so hard your body will turn."

Worshiping the Lord our God

Music has been a constant presence in the life of mankind. One of the most moving stories in the Bible is recorded in *2 Chronicles 29* where Hezekiah restored worship in the Temple of God. First, he commanded the Levites to cleanse the temple. When that was accomplished, they prepared seven bulls, seven rams, seven lambs, and seven male goats for a sin offering for the kingdom, for the sanctuary, and for Judah.

After they sacrificed the animals, Hezekiah stationed the Levites in the house of the Lord with cymbals, with stringed instruments, and with harps, *according to the commandment* of David, of Gad the King's *seer*, and of Nathan the *prophet*; for thus was *the commandment of the Lord* by His prophets.

2 Chronicles 29:27
Then Hezekiah commanded them to offer the burnt offering

on the altar. *And when the burnt offering began, the song of the Lord also began, with the trumpets and with the instruments of David king of Israel.*

So all the assembly worshipped, the singers sang, and trumpeters sounded; all of this continued until the burnt offering was finished. *(Exodus 15:1b-4)*

Songs with and without instruments have been a part of the life of mankind for thousands of years. There was the song of Moses:

"I will sing to the Lord, for He has triumphed gloriously! The horse and its rider He has thrown into the sea! The Lord is my strength and my song, and He has become my salvation; He is my God and I will praise Him. The Lord is a man of war; The Lord is His name."

The songs of the days in the Old Testament were songs of telling and re-telling the power and might of God Almighty. Songs were written of His victories over the nations of the world, and songs of kindness and mercy to those who love Him and are obedient to His word.

Another example is the song of Miriam

Exodus 15:17
Sing to the Lord, for He has triumphed gloriously! The horse and its rider He has thrown into the sea.

And then there are the songs/prayers of David and psalters that are recorded in the Book of Psalms. Below are a just a few examples of praising and singing songs to the Lord our God.

Psalms 103:1
Bless the Lord, O my soul; and all that is within me, bless His holy name.

and

Psalms 101:1
I will sing of mercy and praise to You, O Lord, I will sing praises.

and

Psalms 98:1
Oh sing to the Lord a new song! For He has done marvelous things.

and

Psalms 97:1
The Lord reigns; let the earth rejoice; let the multitude of isles be glad.

and

Psalms 107:1
Oh give thanks to the Lord, for He is good! For His mercy endures forever.

and

Psalms 34:1-3
I will bless the Lord at all times; His praise shall continually be in my mouth. My soul shall make its boast in the Lord; the humble shall hear of it and be glad. Oh, magnify the Lord with me, and let us exalt His name together.

and

(Sometimes when you are drunk in the Spirit of God, you will get songs like; "Humble yourself before God.")

"Humble yourself before God. Humble yourself and all that you are. Humble yourself before God. Humble yourself; bow down to the king of your heart. We praise You Lord – Elohim. May our praise and adoration put a smile in Your heart. For You oh Lord, is God and King

We humble our hearts and let our praises ring. We exalt You Lord with this song that we sing. Jehovah You are everything."
- *Michael Hicks 2003*

When we as the children and Church of our Lord praise and worship Him, we are paying homage, tribute, reverence, honor, and great respect to the Lord our God. We honor Him for Who He is and for what He has done in our lives. The children of Israel praised Him because His Name is great and there is no other. They worshipped Him for His *deliverance* and His *victories* in battle. They praised and worshipped Him for His *provision*, *protection* and His loving *care* that He has often *demonstrated* throughout the years of their lives. As Christians, we praise Him for the same reasons as the saints of old; however, we especially praise Him for *salvation* from the kingdom of Darkness through His Son Jesus the Christ.

Psalms 150
Praise the Lord! Praise Him in His sanctuary; praise Him in His mighty firmament! Praise Him for His mighty acts; Praise Him according to His excellent greatness! Praise Him with the sound of the trumpet; praise Him with the lute and harp! Praise Him with the timbrel and dance; praise Him with stringed instruments and flutes! Praise Him with loud symbols; praise Him with clashing symbols! Let everything that has breath praise the Lord. Praise the Lord!

Colossians 3:16-17
Let the word of Christ dwell in you richly in all wisdom, teaching and admonishing one another one another in psalms and hymns and spiritual songs, singing with grace in your hearts to

the Lord. And whatever you do in word or deed, do all in the name of the Lord Jesus, giving thanks to God the Father through Him.

Praising the Lord is one of the most exhilarating acts of worship we can do to show our appreciation of God's care for us. When we praise and worship the Lord with our hearts, we are very close to Him and He blesses us with His presence. And in His presence is the most powerful, wonderful, exhilarating, magnificent and delightful experiences that we can ever experience. When we worship Him for Who He is and what He has done for us with sincerity, the *atmosphere* gets so thick and *awesome* it is almost *scary*. I am not talking about being afraid, it is just something so awesome, there aren't any words to adequately express the feeling of the atmosphere that comes in *His presence*.

It is truly a beautiful thing when *corporate* worship from the choir or the praise team is in one mind and *one accord* praising and worshipping the Lord. When the anointing *flows,* hearts are touched and Christ is *revealed* in the hearts and minds of men and women. When the church sings love songs to the Lord of Host, the Holy Spirit *refills, replenishes* and *renews* each and every member who is in tune with praising the Lord in Spirit and in truth. When the praise and worship is there – Emmanuel is there.

We should also have *private* times worshipping the Lord every day. There is strength in our walk when we break away from the hustle and bustle the world provides, and *tune in* and *focus* on the King of kings and the Lord of lords. There have been times when I would break away and spend *hours* praying in the Spirit, writing songs and singing them to Him. When we get into the *attitude* of praise - thanking Him and praising Him, mere words really cannot describe the *atmosphere* it *produces*. Sometimes I would be giddy, and happy to the point of tears when the *presence* of God enveloped me. There have been times when the *experience* is so strong I thought I might explode in His goodness. It is here where Scripture is *illuminated* and *revealed*. Spiritual matters that were once hidden are now made *known*. It is here where I can get a *deeper revelation* of Christ. Christ is revealed when I read and study His Word, but when I sing praises to Him, *things happen.* We are blessed when we are in prayer and sing praises to Him in the *quiet* time you have reserved for Him. It is truly wonderful and as a drowning man seeks air, we must seek Christ both corporately and individually.

There is strength, and tears of joy and confidence as the flooding of the Father's love *cloaks* and *envelopes* you during these sessions, and you will find yourself growing in the Spirit of God. Your will find your faith in Him stronger than ever. *Where the Spirit of the Lord is; there is liberty.* There is liberty to *learn* of Him, liberty to *know* Him better, and the liberty to *love* Him because He has revealed Himself to you.

Satan hates it when Christians spend time with the Father. There is nothing he could do about it, *for greater is He that is in you than he that is in the world.* So what he goes after the others and tries to manipulate other Christians into praising him instead of God. His biggest and most successful avenue for this is music.

Notes:

Chapter 13

Demons

There are myriad's of *demons* in the world today. Demons are *fallen angels* who have agreed to establish themselves with Satan to rebel against God. *Satan* means adversary, enemy, foe, or challenger; and his followers have the same war plan as their *evil* master. Their primary objective is to destroy mankind; if they cannot destroy mankind, they will attempt to take peace and harmony away and to replace it with anguish, grief, misfortune, anxiety, and confusion. Demons desire is for men to be mad at God and they also want to tear men away from the Kingdom of God and be *condemned* with them in the Lake of Fire. The Bible says hell and the Lake of Fire and Brimstone were made for the angels who *rebelled*. However, all men and woman that agree or take sides with Satan will share in their destruction.

When Lucifer sinned against God his name and his physical features changed. As it happen with the evil master, it also happened with the angels who rebelled with him against the One Who sits on the Throne. One third of the angels in heaven *devolved* from angelic beings into demons or evil spirits. Most demons are unconfined and free to roam the earth. But there are some who are *confined* or *imprisoned* who are too evil to ramble through the earth as the rest of the fallen angels. Demons have a place of *confinement* such as a *prison* in the spirit realm called the *abyss*. The abyss, or the *bottomless pit*, is the place they will go when the fullness of time has come, to serve their eternal life *sentences* for rebellion against the True and Living God. The Bible describes the abyss as an everlasting fire, destruction, and punishment; it is also described as *outer darkness* with a lake of fire. The abyss was not made for human beings but for the Devil and his angels, the *wicked*, the *disobedient*, the Beast and his *false* prophet, the worshippers of the beast, and all those who reject Jesus the Messiah, Jesus the Christ.

In *Mathew 8, Mark 5* and *Luke 8*, the three apostles share a story about an encounter between Jesus and demons.

There was a man who was possessed by a legion of demons. No one knows for sure, but a legion is between 3,600 and 6,000 in number. Can you imagine 6,000 demons of hell *running* your life? Can you imagine not being able to be in *control* of what you say, where you go or how you act? This man had thousands of demons dwelling in him and he was carried about by the whims of these agents of darkness. Luke tells us, he was kept under guard, *bound* with *chains* and *shackles*; but he broke the bonds and was driven by the demon into the wilderness.

This demon possessed man did not wear clothes and his habitat was the graveyard. It was not home sweet home for this man. This man had already suffered a very long time in the kingdom of darkness, under the *domination*, *oppression* and *bondage* of these demons, and I know that he wanted to escape his situation.

When Jesus came, He told the unclean spirit to come out. They recognized Him and said,

> *Matthew 8:29*
> *"What have we to do with You, Jesus, You Son of God? Have You come here to torment us before the time?"*

They know the identity of Jesus. They were there in heaven and witnessed His glory with the Father. Even though these demons know Him, His *power*, His *position*, and His *authority*, and they still rebelled against Him and the Father. It is like they thought, 'We know that we will be punished and will spend a horrible everlasting sentence of pain, anguish, agony, and torment, but this is what we *choose*! In another Scripture they asked Jesus if He came to send them into the abyss before their time. Demons, like Satan, know their future but they continue to rebel against the All-Mighty God.

Jesus told the legion to come out and they *begged* Him to send them into a herd of swine, (hogs and pigs), and Jesus *granted* them permission. I want you to notice that even though they were pigs, they did not want these demons abiding in them. They ran down the slope of the hill and committed suicide by drowning in the sea.

The man who had been possessed by the legion of demons, *returned* to his right frame of mind and he *testified* of the great things God had done for him.

> *Revelations 9:2, 11*
> *And he opened the bottomless pit, and smoke arose out of the pit like the smoke of a great furnace. So the sun and the air were darkened because of the smoke of the pit. And they had as king over them the angel of the bottomless pit, whose name in Hebrew is Abaddon, but in Greek he has the name Apollyon.*

Demons are spiritual beings/creatures. They are *invisible* as with all spirit creatures like the angels, the four living creatures and so on. They live in a *spiritual realm* that is just as real, if not more real, than this *physical realm* we now live in. In order to see the spirit realm, God would have to open your eyes like He did for the young man in *2 Kings 6:17*.

When Jesus arose from the dead, the disciples thought that He was ghost or a spirit.

> *Luke 24:39*
> *Behold My hands and My feet, that it is I Myself. Handle Me and see, for a spirit does not have flesh and bones as you see I have.*

Spirits do not have flesh and bones as we have, as Jesus demonstrated to His disciples.

> *Luke 10:17, 20*
> *Then the seventy returned with joy, saying, 'Lord, even the*

demons are subject to us in Your name." Nevertheless do not rejoice in this, that the spirits are subject to you, but rather rejoice because your names are written in heaven."

Even though the spirits are *invisible*, there are *manifestations* of them at work in the human race. When the disciples cast demons out, it was *evident* to the human eye or viewpoint that demons were cast out of the people. The evidence is the once possessed people return to their right frame of mind.

Casting out demons is very exciting. Jesus gave them *authority over* all the power of the demons. When they discovered it, through the acts of casting out demons, they were ecstatic. However, Jesus explains that the purpose of *casting out demons* is to *free people* from all types of oppression in order to *freely serve* God and *pursue the purpose* that He has for their lives.

Demonic government structure is highly organized.

The abilities of demons are:

Demons have a plethora or a wide range of abilities and here are a few.

▶ **They recognize Christ**

Mark 1:23-24

Now there was a man in their synagogue with an unclean spirit. And he cried out, saying, "Let us alone! What have we to do with You, Jesus of Nazareth? Did You come to destroy us? I know who You are – the Holy Son of God

These evil spirits know who Christ is. As mentioned before, they knew Him before time began and they know He is the only begotten of God, His Holy Son and creator of the heavens and earth. The demons were there and they all witnessed Jesus with the glory of God before time began. So even though Jesus had the clothing of *flesh*, *dirt suit*, or dressed in *skin*, they still recognized Him and knew the power and authority He possessed.

98

► They possess human beings; and they know their destiny.
Matthew 8:29
And suddenly they cried out, saying, "What have we to do with, Jesus, You Son of God? Have You come here to torment us before the time?

Demons know their future is dark and dismal. They know they will spend *eternity* in the pit of fire and brimstone. Eternity is *endless*, there will not be any paroles granted, there are *no exits* in Hell, there's no clemency, no pardons, no commutations; there will not be any release in any form of fashion from the torment which will be *continuous* and has *no end.*

► They overcome men
Acts 19:13-16
Then some of the itinerant Jewish exorcist took it upon themselves to call the name of the Lord Jesus over those who had evil spirits, saying, "We exorcise you by the name Jesus whom Paul preaches." Also there were seven sons of Sceva, a Jewish priest, who did so.
And the evil spirit answered and said, "Jesus I know, and Paul I know; but who are you?"
Then the man in whom the evil spirit was leaped on them, overpowered them, and prevailed against them, so that they fled out of that house naked and wounded.

It is a terrible thing to go out and try to do the Lord's work in our own power. The job of the Holy Spirit is to *guide* us and *teach* us in all things. So if we neglect to allow the Holy Ghost to go before us to *prepare* us for victory, then there will not be any real or tangible victories. Trying to operate in the kingdom of God without the Holy Spirit is like trying to drive a car without the motor and transmission. There is no real power in any ministry without the power of the Holy Ghost.

The evil spirit said he knew Paul and Jesus. I believe they know him because it is possible they have been kicked out or cast out before and they didn't like it. Jesus and Paul were both led by the Holy Ghost in every work they did for the Kingdom of God. As it was with Paul and Jesus, so it should be with us. There are many people that get saved and they *want* to do great things for the Kingdom of God. The problem is; they go without the Holy Ghost or *direction* from the Holy Ghost. People have *decided* they *will* be missionaries and go to Africa to save the poor tribal people and share the good news of the Gospel. However, many of these missionaries have died in Africa, Asia, the Middle East and several other places because they were *trying* to do a good thing, instead of doing a God thing. If you are called to Africa, then *the Holy Spirit will empower you to go* to Africa, or Asia, or South America or the Middle East. That would be a God thing and not just a good thing.

Yes! We are to fulfill the Great Commission but the only way to accomplish it, is through the power of God, or God the Holy Spirit. In Acts 16, the Holy Spirit forbade Paul to go to Asia and Mysia. Were there people in these places that needed salvation? Yes! But the Holy Spirit told them no.

The Holy Spirit was not with the seven sons of Sceva. They did not even have a relationship with the Father and their knowledge of Jesus was only head knowledge. Going to places without the Holy Ghost can put you in the same position as the sons of Sceva. It will also keep you from unnecessary whippings, beatings and failures in general.

▶ They receive sacrifices
1 Corinthians 10:20
Rather, that the things which the Gentiles sacrifice they sacrifice to demons and not to God, I do not want you to have fellowship with demons. You cannot drink the cup of the Lord and the cup of demons; you cannot partake of the Lord's Table and of the table of demons. Or do we provoke the Lord to jealousy.

There are millions of people in the world today who try to *play* a *religious game* on both ends of the spectrum. There are preachers and pastors who would be holy behind the pulpit, but *practicing sin* elsewhere. If we are going to be a Christian, then we need to be Christians according to the Scriptures. If we are pastors, then we need to be pastors according to the Scriptures. If we are teachers; then we need to be teachers according to the Scriptures. We are not pleasing God by feeding the sheep and then *feed the flesh* by *participating* with the *pleasures* the world has to offer. There should not be any such thing as a stealing preacher, or teacher, or Christian period, point blank. There should be no such thing as pastors, teachers or Christians sodomizing, or molesting children. There should be no such thing as a Pastor lying to his congregation to *obtain* money or prestige. These acts are sacrifices to demons because they are the characteristics of demons. Christians are to be pure and holy; so when we fellowship with the lost and join in with their activities, then we are fellowshipping with demons. This has a tremendous effect on the church, because this action causes the church to be a *compromising* church. A compromising church will not have a place in the Kingdom of God.

▶ They instigate deceit.
1 Timothy 4:1
Now the Spirit expressly says that in latter times some will depart from the faith giving heed to deceiving spirits and doctrines of demons.

Demons have been working overtime in churches that do not line up with the Word of God. There are pastors who do not wait on the Lord, or seek the Lord for guidance. They speak what others want them to say. These others love the *easy, feel good* message that does not address issues in the church such as sin. Others feel we need a *new* Gospel, something that will reach certain age groups, genders, or ethnic groups. So then the Gospel is *mixed* with the social ideas from the world in order to have *success.* Some preach *another* Jesus Who has flaws in order to identify with sinners. Some have the idea; Jesus and Mary Magdalene had children and the heirs of this union will rise up through the ranks of government and rule the world at some point in time. There are billions of *ideas* but there is only one objective, demons want to feed the sheep *poison* to keep the church powerless.

Demons have personalities, they are *intelligent* and they have *superhuman* strength. They have been called Spirits of Infirmities, or Deaf and Dumb Spirits. There are *lying* spirits and *religious* spirits and so forth. They are able to conduct conversation with people as they did with Jesus and also with the seven sons of Sceva, *(Act. 19:14)*. They are also able to *force* themselves on people who are not saved and baptized into the Body of Christ and *cause* them to act certain ways. You see the results of this on the news every day.

The demons which have a lot of *influence* in the United States are *fleshly* in nature. The *pride* of being the most *powerful* nation in the world has many *drunk* in seeking *power* of their *own*. The land of the free and the home of the brave has *detoured* many from the kingdom of God. Like the Pharisees of old, Americans as individuals have become *their own* man with little need for God.

The American Dream has activated voluminous demons to direct her citizens through the media and radio where numerous people are influenced by the news or the gossip of the day. *Opinions* are formed through personalities that possess a charismatic flare to *sway* the masses to a line of *thinking* which is often - *self*. In this, the love of many has grown cold, people pay to be *brainwashed* and find themselves tossed to and fro with every *idea* that comes down the pike. Whether it is food, automobiles, household appliances, or flesh enhancing products, Americans pay millions of dollars to obtain their *luxury* in living. There is nothing wrong with good living, but when it takes the place of the Great Commission, there is a problem.

Sex is the most profitable element in the United States. Instead of sex being used for procreation, it has become a recreational sport in which both genders apply themselves in a never ending attempt attempt to satisfy the *lust of the flesh*. From DVD pornos, to phone sex to the sex slave trade, to television commercials, sex sells. Sex sells washing machines, hamburgers, screwdrivers, cars, vacation oasis, dog food, television shows, movies and plays. It won't be too long before the United States *devolves* herself into a new aged *Sodom* and *Gomorrah*.

It is unfortunate that demons have such a lock on areas like these.

At the end of the age, when Jesus comes back, all these: *demons, principalities, rulers of darkness, powers, territorial spirits, false gods,* and *Satan himself,* who has influenced the people of the earth, will bow down at the feet of Jesus and say, He is Lord.

Some of the instruments of these demons are practices such as soothsaying. *Soothsaying* is the same as *divination* and it is the art of obtaining unlawful knowledge of the future. The *medium* is under the direct influence of evil spirits. In this age, divination is displayed in a good light. We see this mostly from Hollywood portraying good *witches* and moral *warlocks.* They call it the battle between good and evil, when in essence it is evil verses evil. In God's eyes, there is no such thing as a good witch or a righteous warlock. They are an abomination to Him. An *abomination* is an outrage, repugnance, a disgrace, an eyesore, hatred, dislike, and an atrocity. *Spiritism séances* are today's term for soothsaying. It is obtaining information from the dead. This is also called *necromancy.* These are Satan's attempts to dilute the Word of God and gain more followers to accompany him to the pits of hell, fire and brimstone.

Sorcery is the practice of *magic* through *occult formulas, incantations,* and *mystic mutterings.* And a charmer is a *sorcerer* who performs *supernatural* feats. The Bible tells us *sorcery* is a form of *witchcraft* and drug abuse, both legal and illegal.

Occultism involves dealing with *demonic forces* through *fortunetelling, magic, Spiritism,* or fake religious *cults,* these are considered *idolatry* to God. The Word says that no idolater will have any inheritance in the Kingdom of God

▶ Demons also alienate men from God.

Cults steel the unbeliever against the Gospel and use him to resist the Word and harden his heart in *unbelief* and *rebellion.* *(See 1 Tim. 4:1 and 1 Jo. 2:1-3)*

Occult practice results in *subjection* to the powers of darkness. This means that the person is *allowing* himself to be *used* by Satan's organization for unholy use. When the person gives themselves over to this, then the mind is *blinded* to the truth and that person is immersed in *deception* and *error* like Jim Jones, David Koresh, Heaven's Gate, and thousands, if not millions of other false religious cults.

▶ **Demons can oppress the body of man.**
Mark 9:25
When Jesus saw that the people came running together, He rebuked the unclean spirit, saying to it: Deaf and Dumb spirit, I command you to come out of him and enter him no more!"

Sometimes, there is nothing wrong with people physically who are *impaired* in some form or fashion. But here in this passage of Scripture, the person was deaf and dumb; he could not speak nor talk because he was *oppressed* by demons. In other words, the demon was holding him back from a normal lifestyle of talking and hearing. By the same token, I believe many people in insane asylums are oppressed by demons because this is what they do. *(See also Matt. 9:32-33; 12:12 and Lk. 13:11-17)*

In any event, Demons are operating at full capacity around the world and it will not get any better, it will get worse and worse until Jesus comes back for His Church.

Notes:

Chapter 14
Principalities

The American Heritage Dictionary defines *principalities* as:
1. A territory ruled by a prince or from which a prince derives his title
2. The position, authority, or jurisdiction of a prince; sovereignty

The Greek word for *principalities* is '*arch*' which means chief or ruler. These are ruling devils/evil spirits which have administrative, managerial, or exclusive authority or governmental rule in the world. This set of powerful evil spirits *rules over* a particular nation, a specific people or race. For example, these principalities were ruling over Germany in the days of Hitler. He was a puppet for these high ranking evil spirits and was led to do great damage to the children of Israel. Hitler claimed to be a Christian, but his fruit demonstrated he was a *thief*, a *murderer* and a *liar*. In any event, his claim on his spiritual status caused others to stumble much like the Crusaders and the Ku Klux Klan.

There are some demons that are *in charge* of geographical areas, territorial spirits as mentioned before in chapter ? such as the country Iraq, Ethiopia, London, Paris, and even the United States of America. Idolatrous spirits have *controlled* the Middle East since the days of the tower of Babel. *(See Genesis 11)*

In the *10ᵗʰ chapter of the Book of Daniel*, an angel came to Daniel because of his words. Daniel had set himself to seek the Lord, he set his heart to understand, and he humbled himself before God in order to find out the future of the Nation of Israel.

An angel came to him dressed in linen, whose waist was girded with gold of U'phaz. The Bible says his body was like beryl, which is a mineral used for gemstones. His face was like the appearance of lightning and his eyes were like torches of fire. His arms and feet were the color of burnished bronze and the sound of his voice was like the voices of millions.

He told Daniel he had come to explain things to him, but was withstood for 21 days fighting the *kings of Persia.* He was not fighting the human kingdom of Persia, but the *spiritual kingdom* of Persia. These are called twin kingdoms; there is a spiritual kingdom of Persia and an earthly kingdom of Persia. There is a spiritual kingdom of the United States and an earthly kingdom named the United States. Every earthly country, kingdom, and nation in the world has a *spiritual counterpart* in the *spirit realm.* Persia was a world power in these particular days of Daniel. But when the fullness of time came, Persia was defeated by Greece. After the angel shared with Daniel he mentioned that the kingdom of Greece was next. And so it was, Greece defeated Persia in 479 BC.

So we need to understand that each nation on the planet has a principality who answers to the devil who *rules* and *directs* the demonic *activity* which takes place in his territory. All the carnal people, lost people, and commercial Christians will heed the *orders* from their demonic commander and chief to do their *bidding.*

Powers

The Greek word for *powers* is *exousia* which is defined as, 'derived or conferred authority, the warrant or right to do something, or delegated influences of control. These powers would include all high-ranking, evil supernatural powers, the power of sin and evil that is operating in the world. The fruits of the influence of these can be seen in drug cartels, gross poverty, epidemics, terrorism, and other atrocious crimes against humankind, and even toward the animal kingdom.

Spiritual Host of Wickedness in high places

The Greek word for *wickedness* is ponēria and it means *depravity* and particularly in the sense of malice, spite, hatred, cruelty, meanness, and nastiness, this also includes mischief, plots, sins, and iniquity or immorality.

Malice is defined as:

1. A desire to harm others or to see others suffer; extreme ill will or spite
2. Law – The intent, without cause or reason, to commit a wrongful act that will result in harm to another

All these evil *entities* take their assignments from Satan. These *assignments* are directed to attack mankind. These foul, malevolent, vindictive, malicious, and nasty entities work damage, injury, trouble, harm, mischief, and pure unadulterated evil in our world. These *demonic powers* hate mankind, but they hate Christians even more so.

They are *assigned to hinder* the church, to *steal* from the church, and if possible *kill* the church. Their biggest desire is to *destroy* man's relationship with God because God created us and He loves us. Whatever God loves, demons hate.

The Church is the body of Christ both individually and corporately. Demons use the *flesh* most of time to *distract* the sons and daughters of God from their purpose in life and God's purpose for the Kingdom. Demons are adept in both ends of the spectrum in trying to influence men to *rebel* against God. From the usual sins such as idolatry, murder, sexual immorality, and disobedience that are at the one end of the spectrum, to religious piety at the other end, who teach and preach in the spirit of error to *nullify* the power of God in the Church.

For instance, demons are *assigned* to churches to disrupt any move of God, they will use any means necessary to accomplish their tasks. They will work through any *open door* that they can find. An open door is a person who does not have a relationship with God, who does not commune with Him nor operate in the Holy Spirit. So demons themselves go to church, looking for someone they may devour in order cause havoc in the body of Christ.

An example of this is when; a person goes to church and through careful scrutiny, *looks for* shortcomings in the congregation. When he finds something, he or she will go to someone in the church and make *comments* about the person. Most likely, the person hearing the comment will look or investigate to see if there is any evidence of truth in the statement. At this point, the focus is no longer on worshipping God but *finding fault* in a member of the church. This process has often escalated into *gossip* and *backbiting* and will sometimes have the propensity to *tear* a church apart.

A lot of times we see in movies that demons cannot go to church or walk on hallow ground. But that is not true, it is a lie from the pit of Hell. Demons can go anywhere; *they even go to church* also.

Notes:

Chapter 15

Israel's Blasphemous Worship

This is one of the saddest stories you will find is in the Bible. It is found is *Ezekiel* chapter 8.

> *Ezekiel 8:7-12*
> *So He brought me to the door of the court; and when I looked, there was a hole in the wall.*
> *Then He said to me, "Son of man, dig into the wall"; and when I dug into the wall, there was a door. And He said to me, "Go in, and see the wicked abominations which they are doing there."*
> *So I went in and saw, and there – every sort of creeping thing, abominable beast, and all the idols of the house of Israel, portrayed all around the wall. And there stood before them seventy men of the elders of the house of Israel, and in their midst stood Jaazaniah the son of Shaphan. Each man had a censer in his hand, and a thick cloud of incense went up.*
> *Then He said to me, "Son of man, have you seen what the elders of the house of Israel do in the dark, every man in the room of his idols? For they say, 'The Lord does not see us, the Lord has forsaken the land."*

One day Ezekiel was sitting in his house with the elders of Judah. The hand of God *fell* upon him and took him by the lock of his hair and the Spirit *lifted* him up between heaven and earth and *showed* him an idol which sat at the north gate of the inner court. The Bible says this action provokes God to jealousy. Then the Spirit *took* him to a hole in the wall and *told* Ezekiel to dig in the hole to see greater abominations. So Ezekiel did what the Spirit of the Lord told him. Inside the room, there were seventy elders of Israel with every sort of creeping thing, abominable beast, and all the idols of the house of Israel, portrayed all around the walls. And in the midst of them was Jaazaniah the son of Shapan. Each man had a censer in his hand, and *a thick cloud* of incense went up.

In another room, the women were weeping for Tammuz. Tammuz was a fertility god and the women were crying out to the idol because either, they had no children or the crops were failing. When the land was scorched in August and September, Tammuz was thought to die with the scorched land. His worshippers would wail over his death in hopes of his resurrection.

The Spirit brought him to another room and at the door of the temple, between the porch and the altar, there were about twenty-five men with their backs toward the temple of the Lord and their faces toward the east, they were *worshiping* the rising sun in the east.

The elders were in the *dark* practicing their *secret* behavior. They *thought* of God as a limited god, in human terms as their neighboring nations *viewed* God. They did not think of God as being omnipotent, (all powerful), omniscient (all-knowing) and omnipresent, (Ever present).

Since Satan slipped into darkness, his followers also *slipped* into darkness. It stands to reason when the spiritual leaders of a nation *slip* into the darkness, then *the group they are leading will also slip* into darkness, unless there is Godly intervention. When the *blind lead the blind,* they will all be in the ditch. The things that are done in darkness will certainly be manifested in the light.

The elders of the temple thought they were worshipping these false gods in secret. But there is *nothing secret* with God. At first, I thought they had a lot of nerve worshiping false gods in the basement of God's Temple. But then again, it is no worse than going to church to meet women. It is no worse than going with the *intentions* to con Christians out of their money. It is no worse than having sex in the bathroom. It is no worse than stealing money from the church. It is no worse than backbiting, spreading rumors/gossip, causing contentions and strife in the church. In God's eyes, it is all *disrespecting* the house of God.

In *Matthew 21*, when Jesus went into the temple, He *witnessed* the church acting like the world. They were buying and selling items as if it were a Flea Market. Jesus made a rope and *drove out* all those who bought and sold in the temple. He *overturned* the tables of the money changers and the seats of those who sold doves and *said,*

> *"It is written, "My house shall be a house of prayer, but you have made it into a den of thieves."*

When people are doing their bad deeds, God will *expose* them. For example, people who are practicing *hidden sins* such as smoking marijuana, crack, meth, or crank, will start to *show* a few telltale *signs* of their deeds. They will have holes in their clothes; they will be lazy, they will have bloodshot eyes and emaciated faces, they will *display* odd behavior, and will have a lack of motivation. When a spiritual leader begins dabbling in sin, whether it is drugs, women, or selfishness, there are *telltale* signs of falling off the spiritual wagon such as, not listening to godly counsel, emotional instability, and non-dependability and "I, I, I, will be dominate in their defense and conversation. Remember the five "I wills" of Satan. This person is knocking on the door of darkness.

The results of the actions in Ezekiel are found in the *Book of Malachi*, in which God gave the people a pretty tough lashing about the *depth* to which the nation, the priest and people in general have *fallen* from His ways and laws. *Their* pious religious lives had *become* an abomination unto God and like Samson; they didn't know the Spirit of God had departed from them and God had no delight in *their* sacrifices, *their* doctrine, or in *their* way of life.

The conditions of the people in Malachi were so *far* from the heart of God they *didn't have a clue* they were *wallowing* in the mire of darkness. Their hearts were completely *seared* and they were very comfortable in their darken *form* of self-proclaimed godliness. The shocking part of this ordeal is they didn't even know that they were so far from God. In verse six, God asks, "Where is My honor?" The nation as a whole was not honoring his holy name. When He told the Priest that they despised His name. *Their* answer was, "In what way have we despised Your name?" Because of the stronghold of darkness they lived in, they did not realize they were dishonoring the True and Living God. In the kingdom of darkness, deception has a false ring of righteousness but the truth is; it is a ring of spiritual death.

God said, "You offer defiled food on My altar." The kingdom of darkness is a kingdom that is always pushing the envelope. It goes to extremes in its practice in an attempt to *degrade* the things of God. It usually starts off with *small* actions of disobedience and it gradually *grows* into *bigger* and bolder acts of disobedience until the darkness *saturates* the (person) vessel. Just as Samson didn't realize the Spirit of God had departed from him, people practicing small acts of disobedience don't realize they are in trouble as they partake in larger actions of disobedience. Covenant teacher Mitch Mullin says, **"Sin takes you further than you want to go and keep you longer than you want to stay."**

Now, somewhere down the line of history, the children of Israel thought it was not that important to bring a perfect animal to sacrifice at the altar as God commanded. The animal they brought probably had a small blemish and the priest accepted it. This was a bold move within itself. So when God didn't strike anyone down for the imperfect animal; the people probably *took it as sign* that the sacrifice was *okay,* that it was *acceptable* to God. Here is a good place for the old adage, "give an inch and take a mile." Since there was no great sign of God's *disapproval* from heaven, the sacrifices got worse. It got to a point that the people were bringing blind, broke legged, destitute, and patched up runts from their livestock. They were even bringing blind bulls and three legged goats to the altar of God.

Malachi 1:7-9
A son honors his father, and a servant his master. If then I am the Father Where is my honor? And if I am a Master, where is My reverence? Says the Lord of Host to you priest who despise

My name?

You offer defiled food on My altar, but say, 'In what way have we defiled You?

By saying the Lord is contemptible. And when you offer the blind as a sacrifice, is it not evil? When you offer the lame and the sick, is it not evil? Offer it to your governor! Would he be pleased with you? Would he accept you favorably? Says the Lord of Host.

When the *compromised* priest accepted the compromised animal to be sacrificed, they defiled the altar of God. And yet they still replied, "In what way have we defiled You?" In the darkness, there is *confusion* and the people that are *affected* by it do not know 'sic em' from come here' in the spirit realm. The revelation of God had *diminished* and the attributes of darkness was making itself at home in the hearts of the men of Israel.

No one is exempt from the *influence* of the devil. In Ezekiel, he had influenced the elders of the church/temple, the women and young men to worship idols, in the house of the Lord. These *idols* (demons) have *different names* for all the different countries they spiritually pollute, but it is the *same demonic* enterprise in charge of all who oppose God and pushing for the worship of men. It doesn't matter who you are, demons will *try* you.

The Lord's Prayer
Our Father, in heaven, Hallowed be Your Name
Your kingdom come, Your will be done
On earth as it is in heaven
Give us this day our daily bread
And forgive us our debtors
As we forgive our debtors
And do not lead us into temptation
But deliver us from the evil one
For Yours is the kingdom and the power and
the glory forever

Notes:

Chapter 16

Satan disguises himself as an Angel of Light

Another *trick* of the devil is to *disguise* himself *as* an angel of light. He has tricked millions of people to worship him as God.

> *2 Corinthians 11:13-14*
> *For such are false apostles, deceitful workers transforming themselves into apostles of Christ. And no wonder! For Satan himself transforms himself into an angel of light.*

Satan is the Father of Lies and he has been mastering, manufacturing, and industrializing *falsehoods*, *doubt* and *deceit* since before the beginning of time. Satan is the essence of lies; his entire embodiment is *untrue*, incorrect, wrong, dishonest, and deceitful. His laundry list of dark character is very long for he has been practicing these *mischievous* talents and has become strong through studying man and his experimentation in the minds of men. He is the foundation of all that is *wrong* since the fall of man. Through the power of *suggestion*, he has *molded* religions through *false doctrines*; and he is the father of every religion that does *not* have Jesus as the center and foundation of that religion or belief system.

Satan or one of his demons will come to men *claiming to be* God, Jesus, or an angel of God to *redirect* their lives. These spirits will birth a doctrine in men which will coincide or agree with their current lifestyle. The *suggestions* they make will appeal to men because it calls for status quo in their lives, or no change is required as far as the status of men's spiritual condition.

The Christian belief system is the Holy Bible which is the Word of

God. It is *imperative* the Christian man and woman *believe* Jehovah is the True and Living God and there is no equal. It is *imperative* the Christian man and woman *believe* Jesus is the Son of God. It is *imperative* for the Christian man and woman to *believe* Jesus came down from heaven to show us life and to die for our sins that we may have life. It is *imperative* for the Christian man and woman to *believe* we have been freed from sin and death and we are no longer a slave to sin. It is *imperative* for the Christian man and woman to *believe* we are the very children of God. It is *imperative* for the Christian man and woman to *know* God never changes. It is *imperative* for the Christian man and woman to have *faith* in God, for without faith, it is impossible to please God, or *believe* that HE IS.

When a person does not believe what the Bible says about God, Jesus, and the Holy Spirit; then their belief system is false, fabricated, made-up, incorrect, and just plain no good. When a belief system is not God the Father, God the Son and God the Holy Spirit centered, then *a door* opens for Satan or his demons to come into their life and give them something to believe in. Here is are some examples:

• **The Mormons**

The Mormons *believe* that Jesus is a separate god from the Father (Elohim). He was created as a spirit child by the Father and Mother in heaven and is the elder brother of all men and spirit beings. His body was created through a sexual union between Elohim and Mary. Jesus was married. His death on the cross does not provide full atonement for all sin, but does provide everyone with resurrection.

Joseph Smith, founder of the Mormon Church was involved in stone divination, divining rods, talismans, and ritual magic when he received *a vision he thought was God* or Jesus. In all actuality, it was a demon *masquerading* as an angel of light. In 1820, Joseph declared that God and Jesus expressed their disdain with Christianity and the Church. So God and Jesus supposedly chose Joseph to restore true Christianity to the world and to launch a new dispensation.

Three years later, an angel *named Moroni appeared* at his bedside and ignited a relationship with Joseph and gave him the golden plates which became the Book of Mormon. The Mormon religion is named after this angel. The *false* angel giving Joseph the golden plates resembles God giving Moses the Ten Commandments. The kingdom of darkness does not miss a trick.

Here is a prime example of a person who rebelled against the *instructions* of God. Because he and his father practiced various forms of witchcraft, he was a major candidate for receiving *a doctrine of demons*. Practicing *disobedience* in the Word of God will *always* lead down to the road of darkness and *confusion* in which the devil is king. When a person is practicing sin, they are already under the influence of the darkness and will fall for anything.

> *1 Timothy 1:3-4*
> *As I urged you when I went into Macedonia-remain in Ephesus that you may charge some that they teach no other doctrine, nor give heed to fables and endless genealogies, which causes disputes rather than godly edification which is in the faith.*

Again, we are not to teach any other gospel than the Gospel of Christ, nor pay any attention to them. These disputes do not edify the Word of God. The True and Living God did not appear before Joseph Smith. The angel Moroni is a soldier, or messenger in the kingdom of darkness. He is a *demon,* an *enemy* of the Trinity, and he *transformed* himself *into* an angel of light and called himself God.

In the Old Testament, specifically *Leviticus 19*, God tells us to *"Give no regard to mediums and familiar spirits; do not seek after them. To be defiled by them: I am the Lord your God."*

To be defiled is to be corrupted, tainted and ruined. When people *entertain* or *associate* with demons, their life will be *corrupted* with *doubts* about God. This is an early strike of the enemy, to *plant* doubt into whosoever will listen. Their minds will be *tainted* with darkness and will be *unable to discern* the truth. Their lives will be *ruined* because they *did not choose to listen* to sound doctrine.

Jesus tells us *the enemy comes to steal, kill and destroy.* Here, the demon targeted Joseph to bring division and separation in and from the Church. *Divide and conqueror* is not a new adage, Satan has been *dividing* peoples, nations, tribes, and tongues for thousands of years. And he will continue to do so until an angel of the Lord binds him with a chain and locks him down for a thousand years.

In *Galatians 5:20,* the Holy Ghost tells us that anyone practicing sorcery will not inherit the Kingdom of God. The Greek word for *sorcery* is found in Strong's Exhaustive Concordance #5331 and #5332. *(pharmakêia)* The word *pharmacy* derives from '*pharmakêia*' and is described as: medication, magic, sorcery and witchcraft. It also includes *conjuring* spells, and necromancy. Taking *mind altering* drugs such as marijuana, cocaine, and heroin, opiates and others, is also a form of *witchcraft.*

There are millions of people who are *caught* in pharmakêia. People take medication for *depression* and other *mood* altering drugs to *manipulate* how they *feel* only to find themselves *hooked* on whatever pills or medication they are taking. God calls this witchcraft. It is the *abuse* of these drugs that rage havoc on unsuspecting people. When people are hooked on medication, they will not be serving God, they will be serving the medication.

Now there is nothing wrong in taking medication for colds, flues and general sicknesses. And there are medicines that actually cure people and give them second chance at life. There are millions of people who have been cured under a doctor's care and I believe, God has ordained doctors to take care of people. The apostle Luke, was a physician. There is nothing wrong with taking medicine; it is the *abuse* and *dependency* that will get people into trouble.

For instance, in the last days, during the judgments, (the trumpets), that will come upon the earth; there will be people who are watching the unparalleled destruction of one third of mankind. These people are so full of the kingdom of darkness they will not repent of *the works of their hands*; they will continue to worship demons, *idols* of; brass, gold, silver, stone and wood which cannot see, hear nor walk. They also will not repent of their sorceries, witchcraft, (black magic and white magic) their sexual immorality and thefts. These lost people will be so *hardened* by the works of darkness, (sorceries involving drug usage) they will have little care for their own

118

lives. Like a fish caught on a hook, they are *unable to hear* God and will *refuse* God's grace and will literally *curse* God.

Any man or angel who preaches any gospel other than the Gospel of Christ and Him crucified is *not* of the True and Living God.

> *"But even if we, or an angel from heaven, preach any other gospel to you than what we preached to you, let him be accursed." As we have said before, so do I say again, if anyone preaches any other gospel to you than what you have received, let him be accursed."*

Joseph Smith *fell* for the line of the angel *pretending* to be a messenger from God. He did not know because he was already operating in the kingdom of darkness. Jesus says His sheep (the Church) knows His voice and will not follow a stranger. But Smith listened to the stranger, a messenger of Satan and taught Jesus was a separate god from the Father and was created by a fleshly union between the Father and Mother in heaven as the oldest brother of all men. He further taught that Jesus' work on *the cross does not atone* for our sins but provides everyone with resurrection. The Bible does not teach any of the teachings of Joseph Smith and the angel Moroni.

> *1 John 4:1-3*
> *Beloved, do not believe every spirit, but test the spirits, whether they are of God; because many false prophets have gone out into the world. By this you know the Spirit of God: Every spirit that confesses that Jesus Christ has come in the flesh is of God, and every spirit that does not confess that Jesus Christ has come in the flesh is not of God. And this is the spirit of the Antichrist, which you have heard was coming, and is now already in the world.*

I have *tested* this with Muslims, Wiccans and others and have found the Scripture to be *true*. They cannot confess Jesus as Christ, much less that He came into the world in the flesh to redeem mankind. God's Word will never fail.

The Holy Spirit penned through John that the *spirit of antichrist* is already in the world. This was written two thousand years ago. If *a spirit* appears to you but cannot confess Jesus is the Christ that came into the world – you have a *bad spirit* on your hands, an *antichrist spirit* whose only wish is to separate you from the True and Living God.

The following is the testimony of Joseph Smith:

"On the evening of the 21st of September 1823, I betook myself to prayer and supplication to Almighty God...

While I was thus in the act of calling upon God, I discovered a light appearing in my room, which continued to increase until the room was lighter than at noonday, when immediately a personage appeared at my bedside, standing in the air, for his feet did not touch the floor.

He had on a loose robe of most exquisite whiteness. It was a whiteness beyond anything earthly I had ever seen; nor do I believe that any earthly thing could be made to appear so exceedingly white and brilliant. His hands were naked, and his arms also, a little above the ankles. His head and neck were also bare. I could discover that he had no other clothing on but this robe, as it was open, so that I could see his bosom.

Not only was his robe exceedingly white, but his whole person was glorious beyond description, and his countenance truly like lightning. The room was exceedingly light, but not so very bright as immediately around his person. When I first looked upon him, I was afraid; but the fear soon left me.

He called me by name, and said unto me that he was a messenger sent from the presence of God to me, and that his name was Moroni; that God had a work for me to do; and that my name should be had for good and evil among the nations, kindred, and tongues, or that it should be both good and evil spoken of among all people.

He said there was a book deposited, written upon gold plates, giving an account of the former inhabitants of this continent, and the source from whence they sprang. He also said that the fullness of the everlasting Gospel was contained in it, as delivered by the Savior to the ancient inhabitants.

Also, that there were two stones in silver bows – and these stones, fastened to a breastplate, constitute what is called the Urim and Thummim – deposited with the plates; and the possession and use of these stones were what constituted Seers in the ancient or former times; and that God had prepared them for the purpose of translating the book."

The presence of an angel is awesome. Their *appearance* will *impress* any human being. When the apostle John was on the Island of Patmos an angel of the Lord came to him and when he *saw* and *heard* the things the angel was telling him he fell at the angel's feet to worship him. But the angel told him not to do that because he is a fellow servant, and of the brethren the prophets and of those who keep the words of this book. Then he said, "Worship God."

The Bible tells us in *1 John 4:1*, we are to test the spirits. We test the spirits by asking them if they can *"Confess that Jesus Christ has come in the flesh is of God."* If they can't say that, then they are not of God. As human beings we are easily impressed and *the devil wants to impress* us into turning away from God to worship him. If Joseph Smith had not been dealing in witchcraft, but practicing Christianity, he would have known this was a dark angel *pretending* to be an angel of light. The *only* thing God will honor from anyone who *rebels* against His Word is *repentance.*

Notes:

Chapter 17

The Unification Church

•The Unification church says Jesus was a perfect man, not God. He is the son of Zachariah, not born of a virgin. His mission was to unite the Jews behind Him, find a perfect bride, and begin a perfect family. The mission failed. Jesus did not resurrect physically. The second coming of Christ is fulfilled in Sun Myung Moon, who is superior to Jesus and will finish Jesus' mission.

Sun Myong Moon, the leader of the Unification Church, was born in 1920 to Confucianist parents. Moon's parents converted to the Presbyterian Church in the 30s, but Moon continued with the cult. As with Joseph Smith, Sun Myung, Moon *flirted with* witchcraft and *the spirit world* as a young man. Under one of his *trances*, he *claimed* Jesus had come to him to finish the mission of Christ. Do you see the pattern here? Again Satan or one of his demons came to him *disguised* as a servant of light, namely Jesus, and charged the young man to finish the mission of Christ.

After W.W.II, Moon *drifted* from one Pentecostal group to another. Most of these groups had *blended* séances, separatism, ancestral spirit guidance, and a host of other occult practices along with their 'untrained' Pentecostal Christian faith. *Separatism* or *self-rule* was practiced in the name of Christianity. When you are self-ruled, then you are *your own god*.

When a person fills a glass with pure water, it is good, clean and productive. But if a person adds just one drop of motor oil to it, it is *tainted*. It is no longer pure but damaged, spoiled and *polluted* and it's then good for nothing. It is the same with Christianity; you cannot *mix* the Gospel of Christ with any other belief system.

2 Corintians 6:14-16

Do not be unequally yoked together with unbelievers. For what fellowship has righteous with lawlessness? And what communion has light with darkness? And what accord has Christ with Belial? Or what part has a believer with an unbeliever? And what agreement has the temple of God with idols?

When the Bible talks about believers, it is talking about believing in Christ and the work that was done at the cross. Yes, there are different beliefs, but there is *only one true* belief which leads to eternal life with the Lord our God. So believers have *nothing in common* with unbelievers, because unbelievers at some point *disbelieve* God in what He says. It doesn't matter what the subject is, whatever God says is the foundation of truth. It is up to us to believe it or not.

It was through these dark spiritual assemblies that Moon *claimed* to discover the nine levels of the spirit world, each of which he subjugated by questioning the spirits he faced. His *supposed proof* of authenticity is that Jesus, Confucius, Muhammad, and Buddha all appeared and agreed with his conclusions. Finally, Moon faced off with Satan himself and questioned him about the fall of Adam and Eve until he found the real cause of the fall. He claims to have conquered Satan and accomplished what no other man before him has done, including Jesus. According to Moon, the fall of man was first Eve's sexual intercourse with Satan, and second, her passing of sin through sexual intercourse with Adam before he had matured to perfection. Like many other cult leaders before him, Moon brought sexuality to center stage, and cloaked it in religion.

Leviticus 19:31

Give no regard to mediums and familiar spirits; do not seek after them to be defiled by them; I am the Lord your God.

These spirits of darkness should get an academy award for the *theatrics* they pulled to *brainwash* Moon. His proof of authenticity of Jesus, Confucius, Muhammad, and Buddha, could never agree

124

on any subject. In fact Confucius, Muhammad, and Buddha will be bowing down at the feet of Jesus declaring Him as Lord, along with the rest of the world. This is one of the main reasons God does not want us to play or get involved with the occult. They will *steal* your mind, they will *kill* your ability to hear the truth, and they will *destroy* your chance for eternal life. This is what the devil, his demons and his imps do, and this is all they do.

> *1 John 3:8*
> *He who sins is of the devil, for the devil has sinned from the beginning. For this purpose the Son of God was manifested, that He might destroy the works of the devil.*

Jesus came to destroy the works of the devil, not to agree or join in with him. There is *nothing* Jesus and Satan, or his imps, can agree on as far as the doctrine of salvation goes. But that does not stop Satan from trying to convince a poor ol' soul otherwise.

The Unification church is *a chameleon* and is very good at *camouflaging* its unusual dogmas from the rest of the world. They brainwashed their members, especially the female members who are used as instruments in cleansing rituals. There had been several reports of promiscuous affairs between Moon and a variety of females during the formation of the church. Sexual activity is basically a prerequisite for all cults. In the case here, sexual acts with the women of his congregation, and to new members, were used as a ritual to reverse the actions of Satan and Eve in order to cleanse the unclean women. The conclusion is this, in order to reverse the actions of Satan and Eve, Moon had to purify the women by having sex with them. When problems with the sex ritual arose, he married a 17 year old girl and had 13 children by her. They call it the marriage of the Lamb

The best weapon Satan used is to cause *disputes* through *doubt* and *unbelief.* He did it to Eve, he did it with the Children of Israel with the golden calf, he did it to Korah and Dathan in their *rebellion* against God, he did it with Jeroboam and the golden calves, he did it with Rehoboam and the altars on the high places, he did it with

Judas Iscariot in the *betrayal* of Christ, and he's done it to thousands of rulers and kings throughout history. As he has done in the past, he does today. Here in the Unification Church, he *cast doubt* (as do all the other cults), on the truth of Christ and the Word of God. They *attacked* his deity and *denounce* His virgin birth.

> Luke 9:8-9
> *Also I say to you, whoever confesses Me before men, him the Son of Man also will confess before the angels of God. But he who denies Me before men will be denied before the angels of God.*

Moon has passed away but the cult he founded is still alive and well, *luring* thousands away from God and into the kingdom of darkness.

Notes:

Chapter 18

Islam

The people *immersed* in Islam believe Jesus (Isa in Arabic) is one of the most respected of over the 124,000 prophets sent by Allah. They say Jesus was sinless, and born of a virgin. They say He was a great miracle worker, but they say He is not the son of God. They believe His virgin birth was like Adams' creation. They believe that Jesus is not God, and God is not Jesus. They also believe He was not crucified. They believe Jesus, not Muhammad, will return for a special role before the future judgment day, perhaps turning Christians to Muslims.

In the region where *territorial spirits* have been functioning for thousands of years, Islam is one of the fastest growing religions in the world. There are approximately 1.3 billion Muslims adherents in the world today. This may be due to the fact that it is a "submit to Allah or die" theme in *their dogma* in some countries and viewed as a peaceful religion in other areas. The founder of Islam is Mohammad and he was born about 600 years after Christ's earthly ministry. His occupation was a sheep herder and at the age of 25 he led the caravan of a rich widow and later married her later. Mohammad spent much of his life in solitary contemplation. When he was 40, a demon who *claimed* to be Gabriel the Arch Angel, appeared to him on Mount Hira, near Mecca, this dark angel *commanded* him in the name of God to preach the true religion, which ended up as Islam. This shady angel that *disguised* himself as an angel of light told him he was chosen by God to be the prophet that would lead the world into submission to God. He was told Arabs, Jews, Christians, and Europeans had become corrupted with moral decadence, idolatry, hedonism, and materialism and they needed to be cleansed.

John 3:14
And as Moses lifted up the serpent in the wilderness, even so must the Son of Man be lifted up, that whoever believes in Him should not perish but have eternal life.

There will never be another form of true Christianity. Jesus completed His work on the earth and all we have to do is to say yes to salvation, yes to denying yourself daily, and yes to being obedient to the Word of God. When Jesus was lifted up, He took all of our sins and darkness away from us and made it possible to become sons of God.

Four years after the false vision, *he was told* to come forward publicly as a preacher. *The basis of his teaching* was the Koran, which had been *revealed* to him by god through the false angel of light. He attacked superstition, and exhorted people to live a pious, moral life, and belief in an all-powerful, all-just, and merciful god, who had chosen him as his prophet. god's mercy was principally *to be obtained* by prayer, fasting, and almsgiving. In other words it is a religion of *works*.

Ephesians 2:8
For by grace you have been saved through faith, and that not of yourselves; it is the gift of God, not of works, lest anyone should boast.

We *cannot work* our way into heaven. We *cannot buy* ourselves into heaven. If we were to save a thousand lives from death, we would still not have the salvation of the Lord. **It is by faith we are saved.** We must have faith in the finished work of Christ Jesus our Lord; we must believe in Christ. If we do not have Christ, we do not have life but eternal damnation.

- Mohammad taught there is no original sin.
- That Jesus did not die on the cross.
- That Jesus was only a prophet.
- He taught everyone inherits a sinful nature and he believed Jesus escaped the cross but he was executed later.

- Mohammad also taught Jesus faked His death.
- He taught there is no need for a savior, that one must save theirself.
- Muslims believe every other religion is an abomination unto God.
- Muslims believe everyone must convert to Islam or die, Mohammad killed those who rejected his teaching.
- If a person dies in Jihad (holy war) he will be rewarded with 72 big busted women, (virgins) in heaven.

The kingdom of darkness will *take* you to places that you really don't want to go. It all starts with a lie *implanted* in the mind by a demon or Satan himself. Mohammad taught there was no original sin. However we all know that Adam and Eve were the cause of the fall of man. The sin was *disobeying* God and eating from the Tree of Knowledge of Good and Evil. Before they ate of this tree, God said everything was good. So there was no *sin* before the eating of the Tree of the Knowledge of Good and Evil. God said on the seventh day that all was good.

Islam teaches Jesus faked His death and did not die on the cross. The Bible clearly teaches Jesus died on the cross that we might have our sins washed away and achieve eternal life. The Bible teaches *without the shedding of blood, there is no forgiveness of sin.* The Bible teaches *Jesus was that sacrifice for our sins.*

Romans 6:10
For the death that He died, He died to sin once and for all; but the life that He lives, He lives for God.

and

Colossians 1:13
He has delivered us from the power of darkness, and conveyed us into the kingdom of the Son of His love, in whom we have redemption through His blood, the forgiveness of sins.

There was a genuine *hatred* for the King of kings and the Lord of lords from the Jews (the leaders of the council). The rulers were there, the soldiers were there, all but one of His disciples watched from afar, the women who supported His ministry were there and a multitude of people were also present. They all watched as the Romans led Him to Golgotha. They all watched Jesus as they nailed His hands and feet to the cross. They all witnessed Him being raised up. And they all watched Him give up the ghost and die. The soldiers even testified on the crucifixion of Jesus for they made a sign and placed it at the top of the cross which read, *"THIS IS THE KING OF THE JEWS."* They wrote this sign in Greek, they wrote in Latin and they wrote it in Hebrew so there would not be any misunderstandings.

Islam teaches Jesus faked His death, but there were thousands who witnessed His death. There were also 500 people who witnessed Him alive and walking after the resurrection. The kingdom of darkness has an uncanny way of *refuting* a truth while staring at the truth.

Islam also teaches that Jesus was just a prophet. Now a prophet is a mediator between the people and God. God tells the Prophet what is expected or required from them. The prophet then tells the people what God says. Now if the congregation of Islam believes He was a prophet, then why do they not believe in what He said about Himself?

> John 11:25
> *I am the resurrection and the life. He who believes in Me, though he may die, he shall live. And whoever lives and believes in Me shall never die. Do you believe this?*

> John 14:6
> *I am the way, the truth and the life. No one comes to the Father except through Me.*

Islam teaches Jesus was a great teacher, if He was such a great teacher then why do they not believe the lessons He taught. It is simple; there is *a stronghold* in the minds of cultist that is fueled by the spirit of antichrist.

Matthew 3:17
And suddenly a voice came from heaven saying, "This is My beloved Son in whom I am well pleased.

and

Matthew 17:5b
This is My beloved Son, in whom I am well pleased. Hear Him!

God spoke from heaven about Jesus at least three times. The other recording is found in *John 12:29*. It is very hard to overlook the truth, but darkness has a way of turning things around.

Below are a few examples/scriptures from the Qur'an concerning Christians and Jews.

In Surah 5.51 Muslims are not to take Jews and Christians as friends and calls us friends of each other. The Qur'an says that Allah (God) will not guide us because we are unjust people.

"…and the Jews will not be pleased with you, nor the Christians until you follow their religion. Say: Allah's guidance that is the (true) guidance. And if you follow their desires after the knowledge that has come to you, you shall have no guardian from Allah, nor any helper." Surah 2:120

The Qur'an also says if you desire the knowledge of Judaism or Christianity, you will be an outcast and will not get any help from Allah or any other helper. If Allah and God are the same, then they would say the same thing. The Bible and the Qur'an would be identical books, but *they are miles apart.* We are to seek God's guidance through the Holy Ghost. Personally, I am glad Allah is not helping me to understand the knowledge of God.

It is true that each Christian must be a witness to what Jesus has done in their lives. The Lord Jesus gave us *instructions* before He ascended to heaven to sit down at God's right hand.

In Matthew's version of the Great Commission, we as the church are to make disciples of every nation. We are to baptize the ones who respond to the truth of Christ in names of the Father, the Son and the Holy Ghost. But that is not all; we are to teach these newborns to observe all that Christ Jesus taught.

> *Mark 16:15-18*
> *Go into all the world and preach the gospel to every creature. He who believes and is baptized will be saved; but he who does not believe will be condemned. And these signs will follow those who believe: In My Name they will cast out demons; they will speak with new tongues; they will take up serpents; and if they drink anything deadly, it will by no means hurt them; they will lay hands on the sick and they will recover.*

In Mark's version of the Great Commission, we are to *preach* Jesus to every creature, but there are a few things Jesus spoke in Mark's version that were not recorded in the Gospel according to Matthew. Jesus says if a person *believes* then he/she will be *saved*. If they do not believe, they will be condemned, meaning they will spend eternity in the everlasting fire and brimstone where the worm (conscious) never dies.

Furthermore, *evidence* of salvation will be *proof* of the transfer from the kingdom of darkness to the Kingdom of Light. There are some people who may not believe or try to practice these signs. It is unfortunate not to live to the fullest extent of the abilities that Jesus made possible for us through His death, burial and resurrection. This is like having one hundred million dollars at your disposal, and you know you have this money, but for some reason or another – you only used twenty dollars out of your millions and call yourself blessed..

The Great Commission in the Gospels of Matthew and Mark tells us we are to make disciples of every nation. However, we do not force our teaching on anyone. True Christianity does not have a 'join the church or die doctrine'. We all have a *choice* to accept Jesus or to reject Him. It is unfortunate that a huge amount of people will *reject* the Gospel. This is why the road to hell is wide, so that it can accommodate all that *refused* the *gift* of salvation that was *offered* by God the Father through Jesus Christ the Son.

> Fight those who do not believe in Allah, nor in the latter day, nor do they prohibit what Allah and His Apostle have prohibited, nor follow the religion of truth, out of those who have been given the Book, until they pay the tax in acknowledgment of superiority and they are in a state of subjection. Surah 9.29

and

> So when the sacred months have passed away, then slay the idolaters wherever you find them, and take them captives and besiege them and lie in wait for them in every ambush, then if they repent and keep up prayer and pay the poor-rate, leave their way free to them; surely Allah is Forgiving, Merciful. Surah 9.5

A lot of people think Islam is a peaceful religion or way of life. Most of the people who think this way do not read their Qur'an. They will go to the Friday meetings and go through the rituals, listen to their Imam and go about their business. This is true with most religions, even including Christianity. People would go to church and get through the sermon and leave the same way they came. So most people cannot really tell you what the Bible or the Qur'an for that matter says, they might be able to tell you what was taught or preached at any given service. But that is generally how far it goes.

> If the hypocrites and those in whose hearts is a disease and agitators in the city do not desist, We shall most certainly set you over them, then they shall not be your neighbors in it but for a little while; 33.60.
>
> Cursed; wherever they are found they shall be seized and murdered, a (horrible) murdering. Surah 33. 61

In the above Surah, Christians are referred to hypocrites. A hypocrite is a person that has false dedication to God. It is ironic that a cultist would call a Christian a hypocrite. But it is the devil's job to throw *doubt, confusion,* and *offense* at anyone who is willing to catch it. The Qur'an calls for the Church to be seized and murdered a horrible *murder* because we do not agree with this train of thought. God is not a murdering God because we believe in Him. God is the epitome of love.

> *1 John 4:7-8*
> *Beloved, let us love one another, for love is of God; and everyone who loves is born of God and knows God. He who does not love does not know God, for God is love.*

Many Muslims believe Allah is God. If this were so, God and Allah would be in agreement on all factors concerning Bible. However, they reject God's Word about Jesus, therefore they reject God. You cannot have God without Jesus; you can have a god, but not The True and Living God.

The Nation of Islam

This splinter group of Islam has a few opinions. The official stance is that Jesus was a sinless prophet of Allah. The second position is Jesus was born from an adulterous relationship between Mary and Joseph. They believe that Joseph was already married to another woman. They also believe that Jesus was not crucified, but stabbed in the heart by a police officer. They also believe that He is still buried in Jerusalem. Prophecies of Jesus return refer to Master Fard, Elijah Muhammad, or to Louis Farakhan.

Chapter 19

Jehovah Witnesses

The Jehovah Witnesses do not believe Jesus is the Son of God; therefore they *disqualify* themselves as sons of God. They believe *only* 144,000 members of this cult will be *able to enter* into the Kingdom of God. I sure would hate to be the 144,001 member.

Jehovah Witnesses say Jesus is not God. Before he lived on earth, he was Michael the archangel, and Jehovah made the universe through Him. On earth He was a man Who lived a perfect life. After dying on the cross, He was resurrected as a spirit and His body was destroyed. The Witnesses do not believe Jesus is coming back, however they claim He did return invisible in 1914 as spirit. Very soon, He and the angels will destroy all the non-Jehovah Witnesses.

In the first chapter of the *Book of Galatians*, Paul addressed the church about straying from the truth of the Gospel. He said in verses six through ten;

> *"I marvel that you are turning away so soon from Him who called you in the grace of Christ, to a different gospel, which is not another; but there are some who trouble you and want to pervert the gospel of Christ."*

There were some in the Church then, *perverting* the Gospel of Christ; as there are some in the Church today who want to pervert the Gospel of Christ; *distort* the truth of His Word; *misrepresent* the power of His deity; *change* or *downplay* the importance of godly living; and *corrupt* the Holy Scriptures. The people who want to pervert the Scriptures are *false* prophets and they are pawns making more pawns for the kingdom of darkness.

> *Matthew 24:4b*
> *Take heed that no one deceives you. For many will come in My Name, saying 'I am the Christ', and deceive many.*

Jesus *warns* us of the false prophets were *coming.* Some will claim Jesus is the Christ but will distort the truth of Christ. Some will come saying they are the Christ and attempt to inject a *new doctrine outside the will of God* and the deity of Jesus the Christ. In any event, many people will be *deceived* through false prophets.

Then Paul continues,
> *"But even if we, or an angel from heaven, preach any other gospel to you than what we preached to you, let him be accursed." As we have said before, so do I say again, if anyone preaches any other gospel to you than what you have received, let him be accursed."*

To put this plainly, if anyone teach any *other* gospel than the Gospel of Jesus the Messiah, Jesus the Christ, then let them be cursed. If anyone teaches any other gospel than what Jesus taught, they are cursed.

In the sense of the subject matter here, to be *accursed* is to be:

a.   Somebody or something that is greatly disliked or detested and is therefore shunned

b.   Someone or something cursed, denounced, or excommunicated by a religious authority.

God hates a *lying* tongue, a *false* witness who speaks *lies,* and one who sows *discord* among the brethren. *(See Proverbs 6:17b and 19).* So God shuns those who lie and give false testimony concerning His Word.

Satan's kingdom is the personification of darkness as God the Father is the principle of truth and light. Jesus clearly tells us in *John*

14:6, *"I am the Way, the Truth and the Life. No one comes to the Father except through Me."* There are not many roads that lead to heaven's everlasting life. There is *only one* road that leads to God's Kingdom. The rules are *set* and God did not change His mind about salvation, or through *Whom* we receive *salvation.* Jesus will always be the foundation and *pillar* of our salvation.

I have come as a light into the world, that whoever believes in Me should not abide in darkness.

Other Beliefs

There are many, many *groups* or *cults* which have a different opinion about the Son of God/Son of Man. Listed below are a few other groups that do not line up with the foundation, the Word of God.

Bahá'i says Jesus is one of the *many manifestations* of God. Each manifestation superseded the previous, giving new teaching about God. Jesus, who superseded Moses, was superseded by Muhammad, and most recently by the greatest *Baha u llah,* or (the glory of Allah). Jesus is *not* God and did *not* rise from the dead. He is *not* the son of God. Jesus has returned to earth in the *form* of Baha u llah.

In *Judaism,* Jesus is seen either as an extremist, a false messiah or a good but martyred Jewish Rabbi (teacher). Many Jews do *not* consider Jesus at all. Jews (except Messianic Jews and Hebrew Christians) do *not* believe he was the Messiah, Son of God, or that he rose from the dead. *Orthodox Jews* believe the Messiah will restore the Jewish kingdom and eventually rule the earth.

The *Christian Science* folks believe Jesus was *not* the Christ but a man who displayed the Christ idea.

The *Unity School of Christ* believes Jesus was a man and *not* the Christ. Instead, he was a man who had Christ consciousness.

The folks involved in *Scientology* barely mentions Jesus.

In *Hinduism,* Jesus is a teacher, a guru, or an avatar (an incarnation of Vishnu).

The *Wiccans* belief is that Jesus is either rejected altogether or sometimes considered a spiritual teacher who taught love and compassion.

The *New Agers* believe Jesus tapped into divine power in the same way that anyone can. Many believe He went east into India or Tibet and learned mystical truths. He did not rise physically, but "rose" into a higher spiritual realm.

Buddhists in the west today view Jesus as an enlighten teacher, while the Buddhist in Asia believe Jesus is an avatar or a Bodhisatta, (an enlighten being), but not God.

Agnostics believe that *if* God does exist, He will be unknowable.

Animism has a more of traditional form of belief than a religion. They believe all objects contain spirits.

The *Chinese religion* is *atheist* in nature. This belief system numbers about 400,000,000 people.

Confucianism is a collection of ethical or moral teachings and is atheist in nature. This belief system numbers 5,000,000.

The people who believe in *Dualism* believe either there is a good and evil god of equal, or almost equal-power. They believe there are two gods, such as a male and female.

Gnosticism believes we must escape from this world, which was created and is ruled by an inferior and unworthy god, and reunite with the true God.

Those in *Hare Krishna* believe in *reincarnation* and embraces correct living, honesty, with austerity which is severity, soberness, and strictness.

Occultist is infiltrated in other belief systems and concentrates on esoteric meanings in texts, with *magical undertones.*

The *Rastafarian* brothers call God 'Jah'. They believe God fathered a black Jesus and marijuana is used in their rituals.

Satanism is an atheist religion which uses dark and evil *symbology* for self-development and anti-religious purposes. They believe that Satan is not a real being, he is just a symbol.

Sikhism believes prayer, meditation and self-control are needed to become a soldier of God.

Those who practice *Spiritualism* believe the souls of the dead communicate with the living, mostly through *mediums.*

Taoism is an atheistic group that is a relaxed and peaceful bunch that just *accepts the flow* of life.

Thelema is a magical system which discerns true will with *inspiration* from Egyptian gods.

Unitarian-Universalism is a *liberal* and *pluralist* religion that accepts believers without needing them to leave their current religions.

Those in *Universalism* believe all people will go to heaven.

> *Galatians 1:8-9*
> *"But even if we, or an angel from heaven, preach any other gospel to you than what we preached to you, let him be accursed."*
>
> *As we have said before, so do I say again, if anyone preaches any other gospel to you than what you have received, let him be accursed."*

You won't have the True and Living God if you don't have Jesus.

Notes:

Chapter 20
The Kingdom of God

Luke 17:21b
For indeed, the Kingdom of God is within you.

What is the Kingdom of God? What is the Kingdom of Heaven? The first thing we must look at is; what is a *kingdom*? A kingdom is an area or a thing of *ownership,* and is generally used in a geographical area. For instance, the United States has *boundaries* from the Atlantic to the Pacific Ocean; and from Canada to Mexico. These are the boundaries of the kingdom of the United States. The kingdom of the United States has a leader who is called the President of the United States. The President is in charge of managing the country. Now there is a difference between a King and a President. The President is the leader of a country whereas the King is the owner of the country.

Webster's Collegiate Dictionary defines *kingdom* as:

1. A political or territorial unit ruled by a king or a queen.

2. God's eternal spiritual sovereignty,

b. The realm over God's sovereignty extends. *Sovereignty* means *dominion, rule, power* or *control.* So the *Kingdom of God* means God's dominion, rule, control, and power over the realms, (heaven and earth), of that which He created. His Kingdom *reigns* over all things universally including: nations, humans, animals, angels, the dominion of darkness with its inhabitants, outer space, individual believers and the Church. In other words, God is over all things in heaven, all things on earth, all things under the earth, all things in outer space and inner space. God's Kingdom is *soteriological,* which means, *the doctrine of salvation* as affected by Christ.

Matthew 28:18-20
All authority has been given to Me in heaven and on earth.
Go therefore and make disciples of all nations, baptizing them
in the name of the Father, the Son and the Holy Spirit, teaching
them to observe all things that I have commanded you; and lo, I
am with you always, even to the end of the age. Amen.

and

Mark 16:15-18
Go into all the world and preach the gospel to every creature.
He who believes and is baptized will be saved; but he who does
not believe will be condemned. And these signs will follow those
who believe: In My Name they will cast out demons; they will
speak with new tongues; they will take up serpents; and if they
drink anything deadly, it will by no means hurt them; they will
lay hands on the sick and they will recover.

God gave His Son Jesus the Christ all *authority over all things.*
Jesus in turn *gave all authority* to His Church, which is the Body of
Christ. With this authority, He gave these *instructions* to make disciples of all nations and baptize them in the name of the Trinity (God
the Father, God the Son, and God the Holy Spirit). He *promised*
when you preach the Gospel, all these wonderful things would happen to those who *believe.* These instructions were given to expand
the Kingdom with like-minded servants who became friends, and
sons and daughters of the King.

Colossians 1:13
He has delivered us from the power of darkness and con-
veyed (transferred) us into the kingdom of the Son of His love.

When Jesus ushered in the Kingdom of God, the works of the
devil were *smashed, destroyed* and became *ineffective* for those who
are in Christ Jesus. In *Matthew 6:10,* when Jesus prayed '*Thy (God's)*

142

Kingdom come', He was talking about a new way of life for those who would choose Him and the destruction of all evil powers which are against God's will. So when the Kingdom of God came, it gave us the chance to be *transferred* from a life of sin and darkness to the life of Christ and Light.

> *Luke 17:20b-21*
> *The kingdom of God does not come with observation; nor will they say, 'See here!' or "See there'! For indeed, the kingdom of God is within you.*

The Kingdom of God did not come with a great display. The skies didn't open up and there wasn't any lightning streaking across the sky nor was the thunder rolling, shaking the earth. The Kingdom of God is simply an act of God moving in with His people. It is called, being *born again.*

Born Again

In the book of Saint John chapter 3, we find an elder of the Pharisees who came to see Jesus at night. His name was Nicodemus and he addressed Jesus as Rabbi, *"We know that you are a teacher come from God; for no one can do these signs that You do unless God is with him."* It looks as if Nicodemus had *witnessed* several of the *miracles* Jesus *performed. Through* these miracles he *believed* He came from God because only God was in the miracle business. Nicodemus was also a Pharisee and he had heard the comments and all the nasty little retorts, relies, and responses about the Son of God. He wanted a one-on-one meeting with Jesus, the Rabbi, to hear Him personally. So Nicodemus sought a secret meeting with Jesus without his associates.

> *John 3:3*
> *Jesus answered and said to him, "Most assuredly, I say to you, unless one is born again, he cannot see the kingdom of God."*

We all were born with a *carnal nature.* We were all born into darkness. We were *natural* born sinners and we had character *traits* of liars, thieves, murderers, and so on. We were *carnal* people with *carnal ways.* We may have been cute as babies, but we were still hell bound *fleshly* children. No one taught us how to steal – even as toddlers, if we saw something we liked – we took it. It was mine, mine mine! No one taught us how to lie. When we broke a vase or a pitcher, or something we blamed our brother, sister or even the family dog. So no one taught us the traits of darkness, we were born in it and grew up in it. It wasn't until we gave our lives to Christ, that we had the chance to live in the light.

The first time we were born, we were born of the *flesh.* Meaning our parents came together and approximately nine months later, here we are. This is the natural order of life; Jesus is saying in order to get into heaven, *we must be born again.* Or we must come up out of this *natural state* of being and *elevate* to a spiritual plain of living.

Nicodemus did not understand and asked the Master, *"How can a man be born when he is old? Can he enter a second time and be born?"* Nicodemus didn't understand the concept; as with many other people today. It is not a *physical* rebirth but a *spiritual rebirth.*

> *John 3:5-7*
> *Most assuredly, I say to you, unless one is born of water and the Spirit, he cannot enter the kingdom of God. That which is born of flesh is flesh, and that which is born of the Spirit is spirit. Do not marvel that I said that to you. 'You must be born again.*

This is not a suggestion, *'You must be born again.'* We must be born into the family of God to be a part of God. Being born again is not an act of the flesh, but an act of the Spirit of God. How are we born again? First is the *desire* to hate how you are living and desire a change in your life. If the *yearning* is not there, then there will be no change. We have to come to the *knowledge* of the fact we are in need of a Savior and we cannot save ourselves. Deep down we know it would have to be God to save us. Then we must *confess* our sins before God. It took me a while because I had committed a lot of sins.

And when we *ask* Jesus to come into our lives and be Lord and Savior, then the Holy Ghost, or the Holy Spirit, will come into our heart where God places *His nature inside* you. It is like welding two pieces of metal together but in this case, it is God blending, or merging His Spirit with our spirit and making us one.

In John 17, Jesus prays for the believers,

> *John 17:20-23*
> *I do not pray for these alone, (the disciples) but also for those who will believe in Me through their word; that they all may be one, as You Father, are in Me; and I in You; that they also may be one in Us, that the world may believe that You sent Me. And the glory You gave Me I have given them, that they may be one just as We are One. I in them and You in Me that they may be made perfect in one and that the world may know that You have sent Me, and I have loved them as You have loved Me.*

When we believe what Matthew, Mark, Luke, John, Paul, Peter, Jude and James wrote about Jesus in the Bible and we truly believe what is said – it *qualifies* us to be sons of God, it *makes* us One with the Father and it makes us One with Jesus. *Being* One with God the Father and God the Son is truly an awesome *position*. Our character *changes* because God dwells in us and we are now *in* Christ.

> *2 Corinthians 5:17-18*
> *Therefore, if anyone is in Christ, he is a new creation; old things have passed away; behold, all things have become new. Now all things are of God, who has reconciled us to Himself through Jesus Christ, and given us a ministry of reconciliation.*

This is where old things have *passed away* and behold all things are new. The nature of the kingdom of darkness has passed away in you and you are now under *new* management; God's management. You no longer have the devil's hook in your jaw, leading you like a lamb to slaughter. You are no longer stuck in sin and always wishing you hadn't done what you did every single week, if not every single day. You are no longer dominated by a world of perversion, but you are *activated* in the Kingdom of Light.

Now we have the *grace*, (or ability) to live a sanctified life because we have passed from death to life. We have God's *divine* influence working in our hearts. A consecrated life or a holy life simply means a life that is separated to God for holy use. When we are *born again*, we are changed from sinners to saints. We have gone from slaves to darkness to servants, friends and sons of God.

> *John 3:8*
> *The wind blows where it wishes, and you hear the sound of it, but cannot tell where it comes from or where it goes. So is everyone who is born of the Spirit."*

We cannot see the wind, but we can see the results of the wind. We can see the leaves moving in the trees, we can feel the breeze *flowing* over our faces, and the *ripples* on ponds and lakes, and we can also see the *results* of strong winds such as tornados and hurricanes. It is the same way with the Holy Spirit, when we yield ourselves to the works of the Lord, there will be *evidence* of the Holy Spirit wherever we go.

> *1 Peter 1:23*
> *Since you have purified your souls in obeying the truth through the Spirit in sincere love of brethren, love one another fervently with a pure heart, having been born again, not of corruptible seed but incorruptible, through the word of God which lives and abides forever.*

When we were first born, we were born in the flesh – that seed was corrupted because it was a work of the flesh. But now that we are born of God, the *seed* He has planted within us is *incorruptible*. Now that we are born again, we are purifying ourselves by loving God and being obedient to the Word of God. The evidence of this is found in our love for one another and living with a *pure* heart. We can only do this through the Spirit of God which now lives in us. It is a marvelous thing when we see the works of the incorruptible seed which grows in us day by day as we walk on the path God has set for us.

Ephesians 2:1-3
And you He made alive, who were dead in trespasses and sins, in which you once walked according to the course of this world, according to the prince of the power of the air, the spirit who now works in the sons of disobedience, among whom also we all once conducted ourselves in the lust of our flesh, fulfilling the desires of the mind, and were by nature children of wrath, just as the others.

Before we were born again, we were dead in our trespasses and sins. We were living and acting just like the devil – the prince of the power of the air. But now that we have accepted Jesus Christ as Lord and Savior we are alive. We have *passed from death to life* because we are now one with God.

For those who have not given their life to Christ, they are still in the kingdom of darkness and are still *manipulated, influenced, worked,* and handled, by Satan and by nature; they are still children of wrath. The children of wrath are filled with *anger, rage, madness,* and *fury.* There is no real peace and harmony in life. There maybe a few moments of a false peace but such peace is as fragile as eggshells.

Ephesians 2:4-10
But God, who is rich in mercy, because of His great love with which He loved us, even when we were dead in trespasses, made us alive together with Christ (by grace you have been saved), and raised us up together, and made us sit together in heavenly places in Christ Jesus, that in the ages to come He might show the exceeding riches of His grace in His kindness toward us in Christ Jesus. For by grace you have been saved by faith, and that is not of yourselves; it is s gift of God, not of works, lest anyone should boast. For we are His workmanship, created (born

again) in Christ Jesus, for good works, which God has prepared beforehand that we should walk in them.

Thank God for His mercy and His great love. God did not wait for us to be good, or to straighten up our lives. We couldn't do it anyway. But while we were still stealing, committing adultery, back-stabbing our brothers and sisters, lying for material gain, practicing homosexuality, killing one another, being motivated by selfish-ambition, spouse jumping, having outburst of wrath, stepping on people to gain wealth and power, and trying out every person who was sexually appealing to you – while we were in that, *Christ died for our sins.*

So when we truly, truly, gave our lives to the Lord, we died but God *made* us *alive,* (He snatched us from the clutches of death, hell and the grave), with Christ and *raised us up* together in Christ and made us sit together in Christ Jesus in heavenly places so in the future, He will show off His church which received the exceeding riches of His grace in His kindness to us in Christ. I personally believe that He will show us off to those who rejected Christ. I believe He will show the devil and all who followed him the *depth* of His grace, the *width* of His love and the *height* of His kindness to the ones who received Christ Jesus as their Salvation, Lord and Savior.

God has prepared for us before the world began –good works for us to do to help mankind find the True and Living God. We are God's *workmanship.* This means He designed, planned, and premeditated a plan for us when the earth was still in His mind. He created us then in Christ Jesus, for good works, which God has prepared beforehand that we should walk in them. It may seem hard to understand but it is still true. The bottom line is; you were on His mind before there was a here.

Blessed

God's love for us is truly amazing. We honestly cannot wrap our minds around the greatness of God and His love for us. The things He has done for us will take millions and millions of years of *gratitude* and *thanksgiving* to understand the true depth of His love for us. Right now, it is by faith. And our faith in Him is what keeps us.

God has set His Church up in a spiritual position most of us do not know about. In the *Book of Ephesians* God the Holy Spirit through Paul explains *'who'* in our spiritual position *we are in Christ*.

> *Blessed be the God and Father of our Lord Jesus Christ, who has blessed us (His church) with every spiritual blessing in the heavenly places in Christ.*

I want you to notice, the Bible says we are already blessed with every spiritual blessing in the heavenly places in Christ. The word *'has'* means that it has already been done. It is past tense. So we should realize God has already blessed us with every spiritual blessing in heavenly places in Christ. The Bible does not say God is going to do it, or is thinking about doing it, it says He has already done it. We are blessed with every, not a few, not a lot, but with every spiritual blessing that is in Christ Jesus our Lord. The word *'every'* and the word *'all'* are synonymous. When we say the word *all*, it means that everything is included. Nothing is left out. All is not a portion, or a part. All does not mean 25, 50 or even 99.9%, it means *100%* and *nothing is left out*. So when we see we are blessed with every (or all) spiritual blessing(s) in Christ Jesus, it means just that.

The Bible teaches us no one has seen God at any time. However, when we are born again, God dwells within us, and His love is being *perfected* in us. This is *part* of our spiritual blessings. How we treat people on earth will show how much God we truly have. If we treat people badly then we have little or no God in us. On the flip side, if we love everyone *as* God loves then we have a lot of God in us.

So then the Body of Christ, the Church, Christians around the world are seated in Christ Jesus, spiritually. God is a Spirit and we are *spirit beings* because we are created in His *image* according to *Genesis 1:26*. God is a Spirit and since we are made in the image of Him, we are spirits also. The only difference is we use an earth suit or a dirt suit called *skin* to move around.

Ephesians 1:4
Just as He chose us in Him before the foundation of the world.

This verse should be a comfort to everyone who is born again. Out of the millions upon millions of people who have roamed the earth at one time or another, He chose you. *He chose* me before the earth was even framed. God always had *a plan* for everyone who said 'Yes" to Jesus Christ as Lord and Savior. This is only a part of the spiritual blessings in Christ Jesus our Lord but a huge one.

God chose you specifically. Before you were born, He *chose* you. Before your parents were born, He *chose* you. Before Adam and Eve roamed the Garden of Eden, He *chose* you. Why did God *choose* me or you? Some of us should be dead, and I am one of them. Reckless, living in sin, the enemy had several occasions to kill me because of the activities I was involved in. Drunk driving and driving under the influence of whatever drug I had over-indulged in at that time in life should have killed me. Having sex with men's wives with them knowing about it should have put me in the obituaries. Living outside of the law and fighting authorities should have had me in the graveyard. But God still *chose* me. I often wondered why He *chose* me to be in Him. Was it because I accepted Him as Savior when I was ten, even though I did not accept Him as Lord? I would have to say that even though I went to church every week and was involved with the choir and ushers, I was still a devil because I was heavily involved with the world's way of living and doing things? Was it because, even when I was higher than a satellite, I would thank God when I got home safely and without incident almost every night? I may have thanked Jesus, but He was not my Lord, just my Savior. I don't think I will ever find that out, until I see Him face to face.

It may be because He knew I would say *yes* and *dedicate* the rest of my life in Christ. However, the Bible says I did not choose Him, He chose me. Even through all my mess, He chose me and you to bless us with every spiritual blessing in Christ Jesus. He chose us to be *His dwelling* place. He chose us to be *His ambassador* to speak to those who are still in their mess so they too, may come out of the darkness.

I really don't know why He chose me or you but *He did*. Before we could do anything wrong or right, *He chose* us. *God knows* the end from the beginning and the beginning to the end. Here is a clue, before Esau and Jacob were born, *God said* Jacob I loved but Esau I hated. Jacob was a cheater and a schemer, but *God loved* him. If there was hope for Jacob then there is hope for you and me.

John 15:16
You did not choose Me, but I chose you and appointed you that you should go and bear fruit and that your fruit should remain, that whatever you ask the Father in My name, He may give you.

Even though I spent decades playing in the field of the devil, God had chosen me before the foundation of the world. He knew that I would eventually come to Him, confess my sins and be baptized into the Body of Christ. I didn't know it, but God sure knew it. It is great to be chosen and even more so, to experience His grace and mercy.

Some folks will say, "That isn't fair!" Why didn't He choose me? It is because you do not love the Lord and you never intended to. The Bible says *if you loved the Lord, you would keep His commandments*. We should *love the Lord our God with all of our heart, with all of our mind and with all of our strength, and we should love our neighbors as we love ourselves*. The Bible tells us *many are called but few are chosen*. Everyone on the face of the earth will have a chance to choose God though Jesus the Christ, but everyone will not like the *rules* of engagement. God knew your choice from the foundation of the world. He knew the *choices* you would make concerning the Kingdom of Heaven.

God chose us and anointed us to bear fruit. To *anoint* is to install someone officially or ceremonially in a position or office. The reason we were officially chosen (anointed) by God is to bear fruit for the Kingdom of Heaven. We are anointed to show this lost and dying world *the character* of God, *the love* of God and *the power* of God. We were placed into this position to speak *the Word* of God so people could hear the Good News of salvation and witness the power of God to change lives as He has changed yours and mine. In any event, we are now on God's team.

> *Romans 8:28*
> *And we know that all things work together for good to those who love God, to those who are the called according to His purpose.*

Just as Jesus' calling was to be the Savior of the world, to lay down His heavenly power and come to earth *as a man* to free us from the law of sin and death. Just as He taught us *the ways* of the Kingdom of Heaven, and *how* to use the authority He *gave* to us as children of God. Just as He taught us how to use His name, and how to *walk* in the light as He is in the light. We are to *follow* the plan God has for our lives. Jesus followed God's plan and we should follow the plan He laid out for us.

So when we find ourselves in a circumstance we do not understand, we need to know all things are working together for the good because we love the Lord. And as we *practice* Kingdom principles as Jesus practiced them, then we will *go through* the problem or circumstance so God can get the glory, and not us. We all have a purpose and we all need to get before the Lord to find out what our *purpose* is for the Kingdom of God.

When we accept our purpose or just take a step toward our purpose by faith, God will supply what we need according to His riches and His glory in Christ Jesus. If we are called to be a teacher, then He will bless you with the gift of teaching. Our job is to *study* and when we do, He will open our *understanding* and make it possible for us to teach. It is the same way with preaching, exhorting, and encouraging. It is the same process for apostles, prophets, and evangelist. *Ephesians 4* tells us that,

> *Ephesians 4:11-16*
> *"He Himself gave some to be apostles, some prophets, some evangelist, and some pastors and teachers, for the equipping of the saints for the work of the ministry, for the edifying of the body*

152

of Christ, till we all come into the unity of the faith and of the knowledge of the Son of God, to a perfect man, to the measure of the stature of the fullness of Christ; that we should no longer be children, tossed to and fro and carried about with every wind of doctrine, by the trickery of men, in the craftiness of deceitful plotting, but speaking the truth in love, may grow up in all things into Him who is the head – Christ – from whom the whole body, joined and knit together by what every joint supplies, according to the effective working by which every part does its share, causes growth of the body for the edifying of itself in love.

It is the Church leadership's job to *equip* the saints with the truth of God's Word to *build* up the Church of the True and Living God. When I say Church I mean all denominations whose foundation is Jesus Christ, the Hope of Glory! The reason for this is so everyone in the Church can be on the same page in *the truth* of the Gospel. When we are equipped with the truth, the kingdom of darkness will have no place in the Church. Just as the devil could not find a place in Christ, he won't be able to find a place in the saints. It is the truth of the Word that will unify the saints and make them strong in the Lord and in the power of His might. The truth is a blessing because it comes from God. So another part of our spiritual blessing is that we are in the truth.

As a natural body have many parts, such as a head, arms, legs, lungs, kidneys and so on. Each part of our natural bodies has a *function*. The function of the legs is to walk, run, or used as transportation. The *use* of the lungs is to pump oxygen throughout the body. The eyes are *used* for vision, the nose for smelling and so on. The natural body never gets confused about its purpose. Each part has its own *purpose* because the eyes do not try to hear and the legs do not try to function as the lungs function. The kidneys cannot function as legs and the nose cannot function as feet. Each part has its own purpose and does not stray into the purpose of other body parts.

The body of Christ also has many parts. **Pastors** take care of the sheep by feeding them the Word of God and watching over them.

He keeps an eye on them and stays current on the state of his flock. **Preachers** proclaim the Gospel of Christ and **Teachers** explain the Word of the Lord. **Apostles** go into territories where the Gospel is not known and plant churches, *preaching* and *teaching* the new converts the ways of the Lord. **Evangelists** are traveling preachers going from place to place *proclaiming* the Word of the Lord. **Deacons** are the servants of the Church and **Trustees** handle the delicate matters of responsibilities in the Church. The **choir** ushers in the Holy Spirit through praise and worship while the **ushers** keep the order in the Church. The job of the congregation is to soak up the *rhema* Word (the spoken Word) so that the members can grow strong in the Word and practice what The Holy Ghost *teaches* through these ministers. All of these are different jobs and they are all working together as one. Each office of the Church is anointed to *operate* in the office God chooses. When each office of the Church operate in its own anointing, then it will be a healthy Church operating in the Kingdom of God and will have *results* or *evidence* of God's presence and approval.

My Pastor, Elder Alonzo Ponder teaches us we should *stay* in our lane. If God ordained a person to be an usher, then that person should not try to be the praise leader. If you are called to be an usher, you need to be the best usher you can be. It is the same with ministers, deacons, trustees, and all the other positions in the Church. When you *do well* in your lane, in your position, God will *raise you up.* Everything I have received, God gave it to me. When I was *faithful* in reading the Word, He gave me a Bible Study. When I was faithful with the Bible study, He set me as Pastor of the Church. We must be faithful in our *walk* and let God raise us up.

Holy

Ephesians 1:4
Just as He chose us in Him before the foundation of the world, that we should be holy and without blame before Him in love.

We should be holy and without blame before Him in love. I know

154

when people hear they should be holy, it scares them because they cannot fathom themselves as being holy. People know themselves and remember they committed some type of act that does not line up with the Word of God. These people live with a sin conscious and not a righteous conscious. Meaning they focus more on their mistakes instead of what they did right. People do not know that they are *the righteousness of God* in Christ Jesus. Meaning they are in *right standing* with God. So instead of focusing on what is right with them, they focus on mistakes they've made. We as Christians must know that we are the righteousness of God in Christ. We must know this is a gift because we cannot, under any circumstances obtain this righteousness on our own.

A free gift is a free *gift*. If a person came to you and *offered* you a new Buick Enclave and told you it was a *free gift*. You would probably take it. I know my wife would. You would not have to pay anything to obtain it because it was *free*. But if you pulled out your wallet to give him $300, then it would no longer be a free gift – it would just be a great deal on an Enclave. It is the same with our salvation, *Jesus paid* the price for our salvation, and *we didn't* pay anything, Jesus paid it all. Righteousness is a gift from God and it is free for the believer, we can't buy it, work for it, or even pray for it – it came with the salvation package when you said yes to Christ Jesus our Lord. When we realize the gifts we have in Christ, we can walk holy and blameless before Him in love.

(1) *Holy* means dedicated or devoted to the service of God. (2) It also means dedicated or set apart for holy use and, (3) having character that evokes reverence. It is a blessing to walk in the character of God. It is a blessing to walk in His love, in His peace, in His wisdom, in His power, and in His truth. We cannot do this without being *led* by the Holy Ghost, but when we *yield* to Him; we can do all things in Christ.

Predestined

Ephesians 1:5
Having predestined us to adoption as sons by Jesus Christ to Himself.

Let us face it; God knows the beginning to the end and end to the beginning. He is *Omniscient, Omnipresent,* and *Omnipotent* all at the same time. He *knows* all things, He is everywhere at the same time and He is all powerful. He has no equal that can match Him in any area that our finite minds can think of. There is nothing He can't do; He can't even fail because He is God and whatever He says will be done.

Strong's Exhaustive Concordance defines *'predestined'* #4309, to limit in advance, to predetermine, determine before, ordain, predestinate.

There are a lot of people who believe when the Bible talks about predestination, they believe God said I am going to save Jimmy but not Sally. I will save Alan but I will not save Dawn. But that is not the truth. God is a just God and everyone has a *chance* for salvation, but the truth of the matter is everyone does not *want* the salvation God offers to mankind. God knows who will *accept* Jesus sincerely, and those who will offer Him lip service. So the ones He knows will accept Jesus are the ones He ordains to be His sons by adoption. Just as God knows what we're going to pray before we pray, He knows what we will do before we know what we will do. That's God! An example of this is the Book of the Revelation of Jesus Christ. In that book, God shows us what will happen in the future and He tells it as if it is past history. Most of the last book of the Bible is written in past tense. It is God's track record and demonstrates there is no one like Him. Whatever He says, comes to past.

> *Ephesians 1:5b-6*
> *...according to the good pleasure of His will, to the praise of the glory of His grace, by which He made us accepted in the beloved.*

Our transfer from the kingdom of darkness to the Kingdom of Light is according to His good pleasure, according to His *will* and to the glory of His *ability* or grace. We could not do this on our own, it is God Who chose us and *enabled* us to become His sons, to make us accepted in the beloved. He did all of this because we believed Him and accepted Jesus as His Son and the author of our salvation.

> *Ephesians 1:7-8*
> *In Him we have redemption through His blood, the forgive-*
> *ness of sins according to the riches of His grace which He made*
> *to abound toward us in all wisdom and prudence,*

In Christ Jesus we have *redemption,* or we have been *bought* back from the kingdom of darkness brought into the Kingdom of Light through His *blood* that He *shed* on the cross at Calvary. It is here where our sins were forgiven. It doesn't matter what we did because sin is sin. If you murdered a trillion people or told one lie or stole one penny, it is sin and we are *forgiven.* It doesn't matter if you were a gossip or a thief, you have been forgiven. It doesn't matter if you were a crack-head, dope-head, heroin attic, meth addict or a pill pop-per, if you accepted Christ, you are forgiven. It doesn't matter if you were a money hustler in the streets or in a corporate setting, you are forgiven. Whatever sins you practiced as a member of the kingdom of darkness, when you accept Christ as Lord and Savior – then you are forgiven. Even if you cussed out God or Jesus, you can be forgiv-en of your sins. The only thing you cannot be forgiven of is willfully giving the devil credit for the work of the Holy Spirit.

> *Ephesians 1:9-10*
> *Having made known to us the mystery of His will, accord-*
> *ing to His good pleasure which He purposed in Himself, that*
> *in the dispensation of the fullness of time He might gather to-*
> *gether in one all things in Christ, both which are in heaven*
> *and which are on earth – in Him*

A *mystery* is something that is unknown to the uninitiated. No one knows God's plans unless He tells someone. Noah did not know the plan of God destroying the world by flood until God told him. Abram did not know God was going to destroy Sodom and Gomor-rah until God revealed it to him. Samuel did not know David would be the first king of Israel until God revealed it to him. On the other hand, the prophets who *prophesied* about the grace that would come to us by salvation in Christ was not *revealed* to them, but now it has been revealed to us.

So God has *removed the blinders* of the mystery of God and has been revealing to the sons, or the church. The Word reads that it is His good pleasure that when the fullness of times has come He will gather all that is in Christ on earth and in heaven.

> *Ephesians 1:13-14*
> *In Him you also trusted, after you heard the Word of truth, the Gospel of your salvation in Whom also, having believed, you were sealed with the Holy Spirit of promise, Who is the guarantee of our inheritance until the redemption of the purchased possession, to the praise of His glory*

We are so blessed because we trusted in Christ after we heard the Word of salvation. Believing in God and Christ Jesus is a huge, gigantic, colossal, factor of our lives. Another important piece of our spiritual position is that we are sealed with the Holy Spirit of promise.

There are many types of *seals*: there is the tight closure that prevents the entrance or escape of a substance. A seal is also a ring or a stamp with a raised or engraved symbol or emblem that is pressed into wax in order to certify a signature or authenticate a document. There is the wax seal and a few other forms of seals. Here we are sealed with the Holy Spirit. This seal is a seal of ownership for the children of God. It is a seal that cannot be seen with the naked eye, but the results can be determined by the naked eye. As the wind blows and you see the results, you will also see the manifestation of the Christian through character, integrity, and love.

> *John 14:15*
> *If you love Me, keep My commandments. And I will pray the Father, and He will give you another Helper, that He may abide with you forever ----the Spirit of Truth, whom the world*

cannot receive, because it neither sees Him nor knows Him; but you know Him, for He dwells with you and will be in you. I not will leave you as orphans, I will come to you.

I know it seems I am repeating myself, and I am. But Jesus told us numerous times to love the Father with your all and to love your neighbor as you love yourself. Jesus tells us when we do these two things in which all the commandments are composed, then He will send us "the Spirit of Truth" also known as *The Holy Spirit* or *The Holy Ghost*. As we all know, the Holy Spirit is the third person in the God-head. God the Father, God the Son, and God the Holy Spirit are One. The seal of God on us is the Holy Spirit. The Spirit of Truth will come and make His home in us and will lead us and guide us into all truth.

> *Romans 8:14-15*
> *For as many as are led by the Spirit of God, these are sons of God. For you did not receive the spirit of bondage again to fear, but you received the Spirit of adoption by whom we cry out, "Abba, Father."*

We know when we are led by the Spirit of God (The Holy Spirit), we know we are sons of God. And we know we are free from the spirit of bondage and the spirit of fear, because God adopted us, God chose us, and God picked us, as His sons because we believe.

Being led by the Spirit is not a schematic, diagram, map, or chart. The Holy Spirit will lead a brother or sister in Christ in many ways. For instance, He told Abraham to leave his country and go some-where else. Abraham did not know exactly where he was going but he went because God said so. Jesus was led by the Holy Spirit and when you read about His healing miracles alone; you will see that He healed many people in different ways. Sometimes He *spoke* to them, sometimes He *laid hands* on them, sometimes He *prayed* the Father for them, and sometimes He simply *gave instructions* to them. You will rarely ever see the Master heal someone the same way twice.

So do not look for a system, just the *listen* to the Holy Ghost and

He will lead you to do what the Father wants you to do.

> *Romans 8:16-17*
> *The Spirit Himself bears witness with our spirit that we are children of God, and if children, then heirs – heirs of God and joint heirs with Christ, if we indeed suffer with Him, that we may also be glorified together.*

The Spirit of God bears witness with our spirit that we are children of light, children of God. To *bear witness* is to confirm, endorse, approve, authorize, or settle the fact; we are sons of God. God said it, I believe it, and that settles it. We are sons of God. We are also joint heirs with Christ Jesus. So whatever Christ inherits, the children of God inherit. Or to point it plainly, whatever Christ gets, we get.

Finally, our spiritual position in Christ Jesus is wonderful. We are blessed with every spiritual blessing in Christ. We were chosen before the heavens and earth was even formed. We have been *reconciled* to God. We are holy and blameless in the sight of the Lord. We are *adopted* into the family of God. We are *redeemed* from sin and death. We are *forgiven* of our sins. We are the righteousness of God in Christ Jesus. We are being fitted together as a temple of the Lord. We are a dwelling place for God. We are One with God the Father, One with God the Son and One with God the Holy Spirit. We are also sealed by the Holy Ghost.

This is who we are. So when the fullness of time comes, God will show us off.

Chapter 21

Confessions

Romans 10:9
That if you confess with your mouth the Lord Jesus and believe in your heart that God raised Jesus from the dead, you will be saved.

There are thousands, if not millions of people who confess with their mouth the Lord Jesus Christ. However, this confession is often used as 'fire insurance' or a 'stay out of hell' confession. Confessing Jesus Christ is Lord is the easy part. But it is our believing He is Lord, that cuts the mustard.

And then there are many people who know certain historical facts about Jesus. However, they believe in Jesus in the same way they believe in Alexander the Great or George Washington Carver. They believe Jesus existed just as another historical figure, but there is no trust in Him to do anything for them now. So how can a person believe Jesus for salvation if they only identify Him as just a historical figure? They cannot. *If* we *believe* in the Lord Jesus Christ as Lord and Savior, we *shall* be *saved*, but we must line up our lives so our confession matches our lifestyle. This is the sign of true salvation.

Romans 11:12-13
For the scripture says, "Whoever believes on Him will not be put to shame." For there is no distinction between Jew and Greek, for the same Lord over all is rich to all who

call upon Him. For whoever calls on the name of the Lord shall be saved.

Our confession must match the belief system of Jesus the Messiah, Jesus the Christ. If our confession is not matching our walk, then we are liars. If we say that we are Christians and support gay rights, then we are liars. If we say that we are Christians and we are stealing, then we are liars. If we say that we are Christians and we are having sex with someone other than our spouse, then we are liars. If we say that we are Christians and do not respect God, then we are liars. If we say that we are Christians and we hate our brothers and sisters, then we are liars. If we say that we are Christians and we have no forgiveness in our hearts, then we are liars. If we say that we are Christians and we are practicing sorcery, then we are liars. If we say that we are Christians and have lewdness, jealousies, outburst of wrath, selfish ambition, dissensions, heresies, envy, drunkenness, revelries, and the like, then we are liars.

Luke 13:24-30
Strive to enter through the narrow gate, for many, I say to you will seek to enter and will not be able. When once the master of the house has risen up and shut the door, and you begin to stand outside and knock at the door and saying, 'Lord, Lord, open for us,' and He will answer and say to you, 'I do not know you, where are you from,' then you will begin to say, 'We ate and drank in Your presence, and You taught in our streets.' But He will say, 'I tell you I do not know you, where are you from. Depart from Me you workers of iniquity.' There will be weeping and gnashing of teeth, when you see Abraham and Isaac and Jacob and all the prophets in the kingdom of God, and you yourselves thrust out. They will come from the east and the west, from the

north and the south, and sit down in the kingdom of God.

We must have a working relationship with the Lord because He is real in our lives. We must spend time with Jesus each and every day. The people in the story above did not have an approving, working relationship with Christ. They went to church, they said amen, they fellowshipped but they did not have a relationship with the Lord. They just went through the motions.

> *Matthew 7:21-23*
> *Not everyone who says to Me, Lord, Lord, shall enter the kingdom of heaven, but he who does the will of My Father in heaven. Many will say to Me in that day, Lord, Lord, have we not prophesied in Your name, cast out demons in Your name, and done many wonders in Your name? And then I will declare to them, I never knew you; depart from Me, you who practice lawlessness!*

I cannot express the need for obedience and loving one another from a pure heart. There will be many preachers, evangelist, pastors, teachers, prophets, and bishops who will say that we taught and preached in your Church. '*We cast out demons in Your name and done many things in Your name*' but will not receive the right hand of fellowship in the Kingdom of God. Why? Because of their heart condition for those they should be helping and because they did not do the will of the Father. There are many *man-pleasers* that are pastoring churches. There are many teachers who twist the Scriptures to fit into the lifestyle of the people they are teaching. There are many bishops who have grown *lackadaisical* because they have arrived and spiritual matters in the Church are not as important as the check they receive. We must be obedient to His will.

Matthew 25:31-46

When the Son of Man comes in His glory, and all the holy angels with Him, then He will sit on the throne of His glory. All the nations will be gathered before Him, and He will separate them one from another, as a shepherd divides the sheep from the goats. And He will set the sheep on His right hand, but the goats on His left . Then the king will say to those on His right hand, 'Come, you blessed of My Father, inherit the kingdom prepared for you from the foundation of the world: For I was hungry and you gave Me food; I was thirsty and you gave Me drink; I was a stranger and you took Me in; I was naked and you clothed Me; I was sick and you visited Me; I was in prison and you came to Me.

Then the righteous will answer Him, saying, 'Lord, when did we see You hungry and feed You, or thirsty and give You drink? When did we see You a stranger and take You in, or naked and clothe You? Or when did we see You sick, or in prison, and come to You. And the king will answer and say to them, Assuredly, I say to inasmuch as you did it to the least of these My brethren, you did it to Me.'

Then He will also say to those on the left hand, 'Depart from Me, you cursed, into the everlasting fire prepared for the devil and his angels: for I was hungry and you gave Me no food; I was thirsty and you gave Me no drink; I was a stranger and you did not take Me in, naked and you did not clothe Me, sick and in prison and you did not visit Me.

Then they also will answer Him saying, 'Lord, when did we see You hungry or thirsty or a stranger or naked or sick or in prison, and did not minister to You?' Then He will answer them, saying, 'Assuredly, I say to you, inasmuch as you did not do it to one of the least of these, you did not do it to Me. And these will go away into everlasting punishment, but the righteous into eternal life.'

There is a day coming when Jesus and His angels will come for the population of the world. All nations, all tribes, and all tongues will come before His throne. Then He will divide the nations as a shepherd separates the sheep from the goats. He will set the sheep at His right hand. These are the ones who believed in Him and loved Him with all their heart, with their entire mind, with all their soul, and with all their strength. These are the ones who were active in service for the people in the Name of Christ Jesus with a pure heart. These are the ones who *fed* the hungry, *gave* water to those who were thirsty, who took in or *cared* for the homeless, the down and outs, the disenfranchised, the prisoners, the excluded and the alienated. These are the ones who gave clothing to those in need. These are the ones who *went* to hospitals to *visit* the sick and shut in, and *prayed* for their healing and *comforted* them. These are the ones who *worked* their covenant for the glory of God.

The ones on the left are the goats; the goats are unbelievers, those that rejected Christ and His salvation. These are the ones who were in cults and denied the deity of Jesus Christ as the Son of God. These are the ones who practiced sex with other married people or someone other than their spouse. These are the ones that strove in controversy and debate. These are the ones who were greedy for another person's possessions. These are the ones who always had a difference of opinion; and caused disagreements who usually separated the Body of Christ. These are the ones who are habitually drunk, intoxicated, inebriated, and delirious. These are the ones who practiced feelings of discontent and resentment aroused by and in conjunction with the desire of possessions or qualities of another. These are the ones who practiced the illegal use of their official position or powers to obtain property or funds. These are the ones who were having sex outside of marriage or with members of the same sex. These are the ones who practiced intense animosity or hostility toward others. These are the ones who taught and lived with a difference of *opinions* or a doctrine that is against established religious beliefs. These are the ones who worshiped some other deity, thing or creation other than The True and Living God. These are the ones who were resentful or *bitter* in rivalry. These are the ones who were preoccupied with sex and sexual desires. These are the ones who killed other human beings unlawfully. These are the ones who practiced spontaneous violence at any given time. These are the ones who used abusive language. These are the ones who had strong *desires* to gain something for personal use, or to achieve something for him/her alone. These are the ones who used supernatural powers over others by use of spirits. These are the ones who took items, property that did not belong to them. These are the ones who were impure, immoral, unchaste, unclean, soiled, filthy, polluted, foul, and sordid. These are the ones who were boisterous in their merrymaking. These are the ones who were obscene, vile and nasty. These are the ones who are foul and told off-color jokes and conversation.

These are the ones who did not feed the hungry, nor gave water to those who were thirsty, or took in or cared for the homeless, the down and outs, the disenfranchised the excluded and the alienated. These are the ones who did not give clothing to those who needed them. These are the ones who did not go hospitals to visit the sick and shut in, nor prayed for their healing and comforted them. These are the ones who did not work their covenant for the glory of God.

"Then there is the church, the ones who were supposed to make a difference in the in the church body. These are the ones who go to church each and every Sunday, but they did not go in the spirit. Every Sunday they can't wait for services to be over so that they can go back to making money or to be entertained by the society, aka the world. Their real interest was enriching themselves, even if it means cheating others, or demeaning others.

"The difference between these two groups of people is that the sheep have the heart of Christ and did not have to be pumped and primed to do His will.   They were happy to feed the poor and clothe the naked. They were genuinely concerned for those in hospitals and prisons, for those who live in squalor, in filth, in shabbiness and   poverty. These are the ones who talked about Jesus to whoever will listen with a genuine, honest, and sincere intent to speak everlasting life over them. To bring them out of the kingdom of darkness into everlasting life. These are the people who lived the prayer, "Not my will, but your will be done."

Revelations 20:8
And He said to me, "It is done! I am the Alpha and the Omega, the Beginning and the End. I will give of the fountain of life freely to him who thirst. He who overcomes shall inherit all things, and I will be his God and he shall be My son. But the cowardly, unbelieving, abominable, murderers, sexually immoral, sorcerers, idolaters, and all liars shall have their part in the lake which burns with fire and brimstone, which is the second death.

It goes to show Jesus shears the sheep and Bar-B-Ques the goats. The only way to *escape* the fate of the goat or tare is to be *born again*, not by the plans of the flesh, but by the Spirit of God. If you are only born once then you will die twice – but if you are born twice, you will only die once.

Prayer
The Lord is my Shepherd, I shall not want. He makes me to lie down in green pastures; He leads me besides the still waters. He restores my soul; He leads me in the paths of righteousness for His name sake. Yea though I walk through the valley of the shadow of death, I will fear no evil;

for You are with me; Your rod and Your staff, they comfort me. You prepare a table before me in the presence of my enemies; You anoint my head with oil; my cup runs over. Surely goodness and mercy shall follow me all the days of my life; and I will dwell in the house of the Lord forever

Notes:

Chapter 22

History

After the events of *Malachi,* the nation of Israel had a rough time for approximately 400 tears. This period is called the Intertestamental Period or commonly called, "The Silent Years."

Israel lost its status as an independent nation when King Nebuchadnezzar destroyed Jerusalem in 586 BC. The world power shifted when Darius the Mead conquered the Babylonian kingdom in 539. He allowed the Jews to carry on their religious programs/observances and did not interfere with them. Judah was ruled by the high priest who was responsible to the Jewish nation.

With Alexander the Great's acquisition of the Holy Land in 332 BC, changes began in the nation. Alexander the Great's version of a One-World Government was implemented by the Greek language and culture called *Hellenization.* He was convinced that that Greek culture was the one force which could unify the world. Alexander permitted the Jews to observe their laws and even granted them exemption from tribute taxes during the Sabbath years. When Alexander built Alexandria, he encouraged Jews to live there with the same privileges with the Greeks.

When Alexander died, the kingdom was divided among his generals and two of them founded dynasties. The Ptolemies dynasty was in Egypt and the Seleucids dynasty was in Mesopotamia. These would control the Holy Land for over one hundred years.

The rule of Ptolemies was considerate of Jewish consciousness. In 198 BC, Seleucids took over and then, Antiochus IV Epiphanes, who ruled from 175 to 164 BC, changed the order when he attempted to consolidate his fading empire through a policy of radical Hellenization. A few had already adopted the Hellenization way of life but to most of the Jews it was a deplorable insult.

The goal of Epiphanes IV was to annihilate the Jewish religious system. He tried to prohibit some of the Jewish practices; he attempted to destroy the Torah and he required offering to the Greek god Zeus. He even set up a statue of Zeus and sacrificed a pig on the altar. These events triggered the Maccabean revolt.

One has to wonder, if the people had repented in the Book of *Malachi,* these events would probably not have happened. The people of God did not respect Him and He allowed these things to happen.

For these reasons, several sects, or denominations were born within Judaism between the time of Malachi and the time of Jesus. The first sect is the Pharisees or the separated ones. Their roots can be traced to the second century BC to Hasidim. These men had a zeal for God but they did not have a relationship with Him. They held on to the traditions of the elders such as ceremonial cup and hand washings, *Mark 7:3.* They were sticklers for the Law of Moses, *Acts 26:5.* They were very careful in outward details, *Matthew 23:23.* They were rigid in fasting, *Luke 5:33.* They were lovers of display, *Matthew 23:5-7.* They were covetous, *Luke 16:14.* They were cruel persecutors, *Acts 9:1-2.* Minister Shelton Dillingham calls this the worst disease in the world – *selfishness.* Selfishness leads to self-centeredness. The Pharisees were *lovers of themselves* while calling themselves lovers of God. This is *deception*; this is the character of darkness.

When a person develops characteristics as the Pharisees had, the results will be outward righteousness, *Luke 7:36-50. Blindness* to spiritual things, *John 3:1-10.* There will be perversion of the Scriptures, *Matthew 15:1, 9.* They had a self-justification before men, *Luke 16:14-15.* They hindered potential believers,

John 9:16, 22. These lead to the *refusal* to accept Christ, *Matthew 12:24-34.*

Because of these characteristics, Jesus called them *Vipers, Matthew 12:24-34.* He said they were blind, *Matthew 15:12-14.* He called them *hypocrites, Matthew 23:13-19.* He called them *serpents, Matthew 23:33* and children of the devil, *John 8:13, 44.* Children of the devil! Yes, because they had a *false* dedication to God, and no false thing will enter the Kingdom of Heaven.

Because He told the truth about them they wanted to *destroy* Him in *Matthew 12:14.* They tried to *tempt* Him in *Matthew 16:1.* They tried to *entangle* Him in His Words in *Matthew 22:15* and they *accused* Him in *Luke11: 53-54.* The Pharisees were very busy during these three and a half years *stumbling* in the darkness while *rejecting* the Light. It is like moving backwards while running forward.

There was another sect/denomination born during these 400 years named the Sadducees. The Sadducees had the aristocratic circles in the society of that day. They were the refined bunch, the blue-bloods in those days who made their wealth as landowners. They were also in the upper echelons of the priesthood in Jerusalem where they gained their influence and prestige.

The Sadducees based their beliefs on the Pentateuch, the first five books of the Old Testament. They did not accept any of the canonical, official, or established status of any other Old Testament Books including the historical books, the prophets, nor the Psalms. They also rejected the oral traditions in reference to the interpretation of the law. They also did not believe in angels or demons.

The first problem with the Sadducees is they were followers of a man named Zadok who founded the sect. Following a man is always a bad idea, unless that man is following God, the Creator of the Universe and the Father of our Lord Jesus Christ. The Sadducees were a fleshly bunch of men, *"Eat, drink and be merry for tomorrow we die"* was their banner. They were rejected by John the Baptist in *Matthew 3:7*. They tempted Jesus in *Matthew 16:1-12*. They were silenced by Jesus in *Matthew 22:23-34*. They didn't believe in the Resurrection, *Acts 4:1-2*. They also opposed the apostles in *Acts 5:17-40*.

The Scribes were the experts in legal matters. They were transcribers of legal contracts in *Jeremiah 32:12*. They were the keepers of the records also in *Jeremiah 36: 23, 26*. They were advisors in state affairs in *1 Chronicles 27:32*. They were the custodians of draft records, *2 Kings 25:19*. They were the collectors of the temple revenue, *2 Kings 12:10* and they were teachers of the law, *Ezra 7:6, 10, 12*.

Like the Pharisees, their righteousness was external, *Matthew 5:20*. Their teaching did not have the authority of God because they taught from within themselves, *Matthew 7:29*. In other words, they didn't understand their own teaching because they did not have God as the source of their teaching. The one who teaches himself in spiritual matters has an idiot for a student. So when the truth of Jesus' teaching came to them, they *accused* Him of blasphemy, *Mark 2:6, 7*. They always sought a way to accuse Him in *Luke 6:7*. They *questioned* Jesus' authority in *Luke 20:1-2*. Because of these things, Jesus exposed them in *Matthew 23:13-26* and He called them hypocrites in *Matthew 15:1-9*, and condemned them in *Luke 20:46- 47*.

These *sects* were born during the silent years and God had nothing to do with their doctrine. So they served God in the flesh where all of their mistakes were made. The concept of serving God was good, but serving God in Spirit and in Truth was another matter. Both sects missed that point.

Chapter 23

Bad Practices

The kingdom of Darkness only has one purpose, to lead the children of God into darkness and hold them as prisoners there. He also does what he can to keep the lost, lost. He fights hard with *deception* to keep natural men in their natural state. Darkness will use the weakness of the men to accomplish this mission through the lust of the eyes, the lust of the flesh and the pride of life. Satan will use every tool he possesses to keep us living in the flesh instead of walking by the Spirit of God.

In the Books of *1 Corinthians 6, Galatians 5* and *Ephesians 5*, there are lists of the characteristics of the darkness. The following are all the attributes with definitions that accompany the darkness. The Bible says that everyone practicing these traits will not enter into the Kingdom of God.

- *Adulterers* – those having sex with a married person or someone other than your spouse.
- *Contentions* – is a person who strives in controversy and debate.
- *Covetous* – those who are greedy for another person's possessions
- *Dissension* – is the person who always has a difference of opinion; he will cause disagreements which usually separates the Body of Christ..
- *Envy* – involves a person with feelings of discontent and resentment aroused by and in conjunction with the desire or possessions or qualities of another.

173

- *Extortionist* – is the illegal use or act of one's official position or powers to obtain property or funds.
- *Fornicators* – those who are having sex outside of marriage.
- *Hatred* – is intense animosity or hostility
- *Heresies* – are those who teach and live with a difference of opinions or a doctrine which is against established religious beliefs.
- *Homosexuals* – those having sex with a member of the same gender.
- *Idolaters* – those worshipping some other deity or thing or creation than God.
- *Jealousies* – is a person who is resentful or bitter in rivalry.
- *Lewdness* – are those who are preoccupied with sex and sexual desires.
- *Murders* – is a person who kills another human being unlawfully.
- *Outburst of wrath* – is one who practices spontaneous violence at any given time.
- *Revilers* - those who use abusive language
- *Selfish ambitions* – is a person with a strong desire to gain something for personal use, or to achieve something for him/her alone.
- *Sorcery* – is the use of supernatural powers over others by use of spirits.
- *Thieves* – taking items, property which does not belong to you.
- *Uncleanness* - those who are impure, immoral, unchaste, unclean, soiled, filthy, polluted, foul, and sordid.
- *Drunkenness* – is a person who is habitually drunk, intoxicated, inebriated, and delirious.
- *Revelries* – are people who are boisterous in their merrymaking.
- *Filthiness* – are folks who are obscene, vile and nasty.

■ *Foolish Talking* – To be foolish is to lack good sense which results from stupidity or misinformation. Talking is verbal communication. So foolish talking is a lack of good sense in your conversation.

■ *Course Jesting* – are foul/off color jokes and conversation.

The language in the list above tells us people who practice these things are in darkness. In order to *practice* these things, one must *act* them out with premeditation, determination, and zeal on a regular basis. *Practicing* means you have rehearsed these actions and they have become a way of life. The Bible calls this, fulfilling the lust of the flesh.

Declaration
"Because of Christ's redemption,
I am a new creation of infinite worth
I am deeply loved, I am totally forgiven,
and I am fully pleasing and totally accepted by God.
I am absolutely complete in Christ.
I am His workmanship created in Christ Jesus for good works
When I reflect my new identity in Christ Jesus –
that reflection is dynamically unique.
God has made me an original –
One of a kind – a special person"

Notes:

Chapter 24

Our Belief System

John 3:16
For God so love the world He gave His only begotten Son, that whoever believes in Him should not perish but have eternal life.

The *belief system* of the Christian faith is what *separates* those who are going to heaven from those who are going to the Lake of Fire. What we believe *divides* everyone between the kingdom of darkness from the Kingdom of Light. A belief system is simply what we believe.

The word '*believe*' is mentioned 118 times in the New Testament alone. It is defined as to 'accept (a statement, supposition, or opinion) as true; I believe God exist.

In Strong's, the Greek word for '*believe*' is (*pistĕuö*). It is to "to have faith" (in, upon, or with respect to, a person or a thing) i.e. credit – to entrust (especially one's spiritual wellbeing to Christ: - believe (-r), commit (to trust), put in trust with.

So the word 'believe' is a very important word, but it is even more important to act upon what you believe. For the Sons and Daughters of God, to believe is a lifesaving gift. We are *blessed* to *believe* God, to have *faith* in Christ, and depend upon the Holy Ghost. There are billions who believe in other things and therein is a colossal human tragedy.

God makes a statement, "*He so loved the world that He gave*

177

His only begotten Son." Why did He do this? He did it so that everyone on the face of the planet could have a chance for salvation. "Everyone who believes in Jesus will not perish but have eternal life." It is what we believe that makes the difference between life and death, between eternal life and eternal damnation.

John 3:17
For God did not send His Son into the world to condemn the world, but that the world through Him might be saved.

The status of the world is *lost*; we were without God and without clarity of righteous living. The prince of the power of the air has been running roughshod over the people of the earth and has ruled through darkness in his unholy office for nearly 4,000 years. The fullness of time had come and it was time for change. It was time for Jesus to put on His earth suit and come down to earth as a man to redeem mankind from the kingdom of darkness. God decided that whoever believes on Jesus, His Son, He would save their eternal lives. Jesus did not come to condemn the world, He came to teach and preach and demonstrate the love of God. He came to show the world the light and to give the world a way of escape, for *judgment* was coming and God wanted everyone to have a chance at eternal salvation.

Israel had over three thousand years to choose God once and for all. But their relationship with God has been *up* and *down* throughout history. They would serve God for a period of time and then they would serve other gods for a period of time. Instead of the nation getting stronger through time, they had gotten weaker spiritually because of *compromise* and being disrespectful to the One Who sits on the Throne.

God has been telling His prophets what He was going to do; so when the fullness of time came, the Son of God to came in the flesh to redeem mankind. He was giving the world one

178

more chance to come to the knowledge of the truth, one more chance to live as we were born to live, one more chance to escape the gates of hell.

> *John 3:18*
> *He who believes in Him is not condemned; but he who does not believe is condemned already, because he has not believed in the name of the begotten Son of God.*

He who believes is not *condemned*. It is difficult for folks not to believe what God the Creator says! Why? Simply because He couldn't put it any plainer than that; if you believe in Jesus Christ then you are saved and not condemned, you will not go to *hell* and the Lake of Brimstone and Fire. You will not be *tormented* day and night, day after day, week after week, year after year, millennium after millennium, forever and ever.

> *John 3:36*
> *He who believes in the Son has everlasting life; he who does not believe in the Son shall not see life, but the wrath of God abides on him.*

However, if you do not believe, you are already condemned and the wrath of God is on those who do not believe and/or reject God's great offer of salvation. *Wrath* in the Greek (3709) is violent passion or justifiable abhorrence. It is *punishment,* anger, indignation and *vengeance* and who in their right mind would want that from God. Who would want to sign up for that? This is what to expect if you do not believe in Jesus as the Son of God. This is what you are experiencing now if you don't believe in Jesus.

> *John 3:19*
> *And this is the condemnation, that the light has come*

*into the world, and men loved the darkness rather than the
light, because their deeds were evil.*

The word *condemnation* comes from the word *condemn* and
is defined as: to declare to be reprehensible, wrong, or evil usually after weighing the evidence of your acts and lifestyle without reservation. It is to be pronounced guilty. Jesus came to
correct our lives because *we have all sinned and fallen short of
the glory of God, (see Romans 3:23)* God sent Jesus to help us,
to show us; we as a race of people are not going to make it into
heaven with eternal life if we keep living as we are living.

But the world *chooses* the darkness instead of the light. The
world chose to be condemned, the world chose to be guilty, the
world *chose* to be sentenced to the second death, the world chose
to be convicted of a Godless life, and the world chose to have the
wrath of God in their lives. The Bible says that the wrath of God
is on the sons of *disobedience* for *refusing* His care, His salvation, and His way of doing things.

The world loved the darkness more than the light because they
did not want change in their lives. They were happy with the *status quo* and had grown *accustomed* to their way of life. After all,
their parents lived that way, their grandparents live that way – as
far back as they can remember, life was lived in a manner in that
they were living; in disobedience, ignorance and rebellion. They
wanted the so-called good the world has to offer, however, there
is nothing in the world that is genuinely good.

This reminds me of *the American Dream.* Every family lives
in a beautiful house with a white picket fence. Everyone's dog
wags its tail as he greets all the passersby's with the lick of its
tongue. There are two new shiny cars to adorn the driveway.
The children ride their bicycles up and down the street while
their Dad grills steaks and hotdogs on the Barbie. And last, but
not least, the smiling gorgeous wife comes out of the house with

an ice-cold pitcher of Lemonade.

But there isn't an American dream. Millions of people want to live comfortably even though the sound of gunshots can be heard from time to time. Life is considered good even though domestic violence becomes a common occurrence somewhere on your street. Life is considered good even though there have been a rash of burglaries around the corner. Life is good because the gamblers, prostitutes, pimps and players keep to the red light district. Life is good even when babies are neglected and children go hungry every day. Life is still good even when the neighborhood priest molested several children. There is no American dream – there is only the reality of God. When you believe in His Son, you may go through trials and tribulations, but the secret is; you go on through them. The reason for all the crime in the world and all its evil is because we chose to live in the darkness rather that the light. We chose to be murdered, raped, sodomized, robbed, and run over because we rejected God's Son and plan of salvation.

John 3:20
For everyone practicing evil hates the light and does not come to the light, lest his deeds should be exposed.

Everyone who is practicing evil hates Jesus and wants no part of Him. Everyone that is lying, gossiping, hating, lusting, killing, stealing, having sex with someone else's spouse, having sex for drugs or money, having illicit or unlawful sex, practicing incest, reading horoscopes and tarot cards, star gazers and serving other gods on a daily basis, hates Jesus and wants no part of Him. Everyone that practices arguments, disputes, contentions, disagreements, conflicts, and controversies hates Jesus and wants no part of Him. Everyone who assaults others in their wrath, everyone that does things for themselves and not for others, all envious, all murderers, all drunkards, and all party mongers hate Jesus. They will not come to Him because their lifestyles will be exposed. The news is; our lifestyles are already exposed and this is why the Father sent Him down to us.

> *John 3:21*
> *But he who does the truth comes to the light, that his deeds may be clearly seen, that they had been done in God.*

There are no personal *secrets* for those who live in the Kingdom of Light. Christians are to live a *transparent* life, *hiding* nothing. It is not because God *sees* our every move and thoughts; it is because we are new creatures in Christ and a dwelling place for the Most High. We have a nature now that coexists with God because we are born of His seed. This lifestyle can only be obtained by believing in Jesus, being born again and allowing the Holy Spirit lead your life. But in order to believe in Jesus, your belief system must be on point. Or your belief system must agree with every word that proceeds out of the mouth of God - The Bible.

The *Belief System* is simply a system of what you believe. The things a person believes make up his or her belief system, whether good or bad. If a male believes that he is a female, then his belief system will reflect that. If a woman *believes* that she is the best softball player in the world, her *actions* will *emulate* her beliefs. If a person does not believe God, then the person will *act* like an unbeliever. People who say they are believers, must believe God and when they do, they will act like believers.

> *Romans 8:28*
> *And we know that all things work together for good to those who love God, to those who are the called according to His purpose.*

Sometimes things happen to people in order for the glory of God, the Power of God and the love of God to be manifested. The *difference between* the *good* results and *bad* results is the *believer's belief system*. Jesus demonstrated this in *John 11:4* with the death and resurrection of Lazarus.

> *This sickness is not unto death, but for the glory of God, that the Son of God be glorified through it.*

The believer's belief system should be *visible* for all to see, just as Jesus' belief system was *manifested* in the public eye. We think on what we believe and we act on what we think. When these two particulars come together, the belief system will be in full action.

If a person would remember that the Bible says, *"Whatever we ask for, we will receive if we believe."* When you believe this truth, then you're agreeing with God and standing on something. If you do not believe, then doubt will cloud your spiritual conscious and you will be not be standing on anything good and you will not be able to receive concerning your deliverance.

For instance, when a trail of life accosts a believer, the Word that is in him and has been growing in him will be *assured* that God is sovereign, powerful and all-knowing. He will know God and will take care of the problem because *he knows* the Word and He knows the *promises* and conditions in that Word, so eventually, there should be nothing in the visible world or the invisible world that could shake his *faith*. He knows that God is *faithful* and that He never leaves us unprotected because he knows that His Word is *true*. This does not mean that the believer won't get tried on his beliefs, because he will. But God's truth says the believer is an overcomer and whatsoever comes down the path to the believer will be overcome by the power of God because he believes it. This is what makes a believer a believer. He believes in God and that

He will deliver him out of whatsoever. This is faithfulness.

If his belief system is shaky, then he will go to someone and ask him or her, "What happened?" They would wonder if God has abandoned him. Or if God's Word is true or this is something that God cannot handle. Most of the time, the person would try to handle the problem himself. He will try to fix the problem in his own strength and in his own wisdom. A shaky belief system will cause his entire world to be shaky and undependable.

The truth of the matter is that he has failed to realize the thing he thinks is bad is actually something that has a chance to *strengthen* him as a believer. The bad news they may think will happen could be something that will deliver them out of something else. Or it could be something which *builds* the testimony of the believer.

Before King David ever became the King of Israel, he had to build his *testimony*. His testimony didn't start when he was king; it began when he was a young boy on the backside of the mountain. He was the shepherd of his father's flock of sheep. David didn't know it but his testimony was being built while on the backside of that mountain, and God was getting him ready for the calling that was on his life. God was preparing his belief system, and David was a good student.

One day a lion came around to make a quick lunch out of one the flock. David took the lion by the beard and killed him. Another day a bear came around to have some fresh mutton, but David killed the bear just like he killed the lion. All things were working for David's good because he loved the Lord, and he was *called according to the purpose* God had for his life. These small battles were setting David up for a bigger battle, Goliath. Everyone knows the story of the fight between David and Goliath.

Goliath made a spectacle of the army of Israel. Israel's belief system was weak at this time. Goliath dared them and even double dared them to come out and fight. To Israel, he *looked* so fierce, so ferocious, so brutal, and so vicious; they believed that they could not overcome the giant because they were looking with their physical eyes instead of looking to the Lord. The Bible says, Goliath was about nine feet tall and was so big that he had six fingers on each hand and six toes on each foot. *Doubt* and *unbelief* permeated throughout the Israeli army. In fact, he had all the men in Israel quaking in their war sandals for no one wanted to take on the colossal warrior. He defiled the armies of Israel for several days.

But David saw things a little different, because his belief system was different from the men of Israel. He had spent a lot of time on the backside of the mountain and a lot of time communing with God. To David, Goliath was just another step of walking into the promise God had made to him. To David, Goliath was just like the lion and bear, an *opportunity* for the glory of God to be *manifested* in the situation. So David treated Goliath the same way he treated the lion and the bear. The best part is that David did to Goliath, what Goliath said he would do to David. Remember, *he who curses Israel will be cursed and he who blesses Israel will be blessed.*

The lion and the bear may seem like a bad thing to the casual observer, but God was using the lion and the bear to build David's faith. God used this to *enhance* his belief system. When Goliath finally showed up on the scene, David didn't quiver, he didn't stutter, and he was not affected by the appearance of the giant. King Saul and his army were fighting men and have been mighty in battle. However, on this day, God gave the entire nation *a lesson* with a seventeen year old boy's belief system.

There will be lions and bears in the lives of the believer. God gave every man *a measure of faith.* We are to use the faith He gave us to *overcome* the obstacles of the world and to give Him the glory. So when things happen in the life of the believer, I believe that most of the time, it is God using this circumstance to raise you to *new levels* of faith and *empowering* your belief system.

"I overcame cancer," are the words of a true believer. Or, "I overcame a stroke or a heart attack. I overcame a life sentence, I overcame alcoholism or drug abuse, I overcame sexual perversion, or I overcame a car wreck." To these people, a headache or the common cold could have been their lion or the bear. After overcoming something small like this, your *faith grows* and you begin overcoming *bigger* barriers, *greater* stumbling block, *larger* difficulties, and *incomparable* encumbrances. The Christian life is one of having the testimony of, "Look at what God has brought me through!"

God loves faithfulness and God loves overcomers. We were saved to be overcomers. We were created to be overcomers. So when the trails of Satan/life confront you in the arena of life for a believer, the believer will ask God, "What's going on?" And after meditating on the circumstance, the believer put *John 14:14* into action. *"If you ask anything in My Name, I will do it!"* When you *ask* according to the Word, you will get an *answer.*

> *2 Corinthians 1:20*
> *For all the promises of God in Him are yes, and in Him Amen, to the glory of God through us.*

This is why *all things work for the good for those who are called,* chosen in Christ Jesus to show the power, the love and the wisdom of God in all situations. Jesus is still the perfect example of God's love. We see this in the way that He handled the people who were hurting. The Bible says:

> *1 John 4:7-8*
> *Beloved, let us love one another for love is of God; and everyone who loves is born of God and knows God. He who does not love does not love God, for God is love.*

Your belief system *determines* who you are and *dictates* your actions. The base of any Christian's belief system will be love.

186

Prayer

Psalms 26
Vindicate me, oh Lord,
for I have walked in my integrity.
I have also trusted in You;
I shall not slip

Examine me, O Lord, and prove me;
Try my mind and my heart.

For Your loving-kindness is before my eyes,
And I have walked in Your truth.

I have not set with idolatrous mortals,
Nor will I go in with the hypocrites.

I have hated the assembly of evil doers,
And will not sit with the wicked.

I will wash my hands in innocence;
So I will go about Your altar, Oh Lord,

That I may proclaim with the voice of thanksgiving,
And tell of all Your wondrous works.

Lord, I have loved the habitation of Your house,
And the place where Your glory dwells.

Do not gather my soul with sinners,
Nor my life with bloodthirsty men,

In whose hands is a sinister scheme,
And whose right hand is full of bribes.

But as for me, I will walk in my integrity;
Redeem me and be merciful to me.

My foot stands in an even place;
In the congregations I will bless the Lord.

Notes:

Chapter 25

The Names of God

Through the Jewish history, we see the many names of God, as He became real to them when they were in need. Or when they acknowledged Him for whatever He has done for them.

Adonai	*Plural of Adoni*	*Ps. 110:1*
EL	*Mighty, Powerful & Sovereign*	*Ps. 68:35*
El Elyon	*GOD Most High*	*Gen. 14:20*
El Olam	*GOD of Eternity*	*Gen. 21:3-4*
El Shaddai	*GOD Almighty, Breasty One*	*Gen. 17:1*
Elohe	*GOD, GOD of Israel*	*Gen. 33:20*
Elohim	*Plural for El*	*Gen. 1:1*
Jehovah Eloheka	*The Lord your GOD*	*Ex. 23:25*
Jehovah Elohenu	*The Lord our GOD*	*Mic. 4:5*
Jehovah Hosenu	*The Lord my GOD*	*Ps. 7:3*
Jehovah Jireh	*The Lord will provide*	*Gen. 22:14*
Jehovah M'kaddeshem	*The Lord your Sanctifier*	*Lev 20:7-8*
Jehovah Nissi	*The Lord our Banner*	*Ex. 17:15*
Jehovah Rohi	*The Lord my Shepherd*	*Ps. 23*
Jehovah Ropheka	*The Lord your healer*	*Ex. 15:27*
Jehovah Shalom	*The Lord our Peace*	*Judg. 6:24*
Jehovah Shammah	*The Lord is Ever-present*	*Eze. 48:35*
Jehovah Tsebaoth	*The Lord of Host*	*Zech. 4:6*
Jehovah Tsidkenu	*The Lord our Righteousness*	*Jer. 23:7*
YHWH/Jehovah	*Lord, I AM*	*Ex. 6:2*

Through the ages, men gave these names to God. Today, God is the same as He was since our beginning. He is the same Provider, He is the same Deliverer, He is the same Sanctifier, He is the same Healer, He will always be our Peace, He will always be our Victory Banner, and He will always be our Shepherd. God is whatever you need Him to be, whenever you need Him to be it. To tell the truth, one cannot simply explain God. He just IS.

The Attributes of God

Psalms 97:1-6

The Lord reigns; let the earth rejoice; let the multitude of isles be glad! Clouds and darkness surround Him; Righteousness and justice are the foundation of His throne. A fire goes before Him, and burns up His enemies round about. His lightings light up the world; the earth sees and trembles. The mountains melt like wax at the presence of the Lord, at the presence of the Lord of the whole earth. The heavens declare His righteousness, and all the people see His glory.

In this chapter, we will look at the attributes of God. *Attributes* are simply: the quality of God, the *characteristics* of God, and the *features* that God possesses.

So what is God like? Throughout the Bible, His Holy and written Word, we see many of God's attributes. For instance: God is everlasting, He is eternal. And as mentioned before, God is actually before the beginning because the beginning has a starting place. God does not have a starting place, He just IS. We as mankind have a starting place. The heavens and the earth have a starting place but God does not. Even the Lord Jesus, Who is the *Alpha* and *Omega*, *(Revelation 1:8)*, has a starting place because the Bible says in *John1:14*, "the Word was the only begotten of the Father. *Begotten* comes from the word *beget* which means to 'father or to cause to exist.' So in conclusion, the Father, God was here even before there was a here.

There are some that would say *John 1:14* is referenced only to His birth, (begotten), when He came in the flesh to live as a man upon the earth. But as we look at the relationship of Father and Son, we notice that Jesus always gave His Father all the glory and the honor that was due His Name. Jesus always treated Him as Father and we have adopted that same manner with our earthly fathers. On earth as it is in heaven.

There are too many places in the bible where they are separated as God the Father, God the Son and God the Holy Spirit. Yet they are One.

Jesus is the image of the invisible God

Colossians 1:15-17

He is the image of the invisible God, the firstborn over all creation. For by Him all things that were created that are in heaven, and the earth, visible and invisible, whether thrones or dominions or principalities or powers. All things were created through Him and for Him. And He is before all things, and in Him all things consist.

Image here means an exact revelation, representation, depiction, or exemplification of something. It is an exact reproduction of person or an object. Here it is Jesus as the *reproduction* of God the Father. Jesus is the visible image of what we cannot see. Jesus tells us in *John 14:9*, "*He who has seen Me has seen the Father.*" They are the same.

The Bible tells us no man has seen God, but if we *look* to Jesus, we can *see* the Father. This is not just in a physical sense but in a spiritual sense. In Christ, we see the *ways* of the Father, the *love* of the Father, the *compassion* of the Father, and the *power* of the Father in those who are His children.

God neither faints nor is weary and His understanding is unsearchable. - *Isaiah 40:28*

God's strength cannot be measured. If we took every power plant that ever existed and every source of energy and multiplied that by hundreds of trillions of times, it would not even be a close representation of God's power. His *strength* and His power are unfathomable, incomprehensible, unending, enigmatic, unknowable, impenetrable, profound, boundless, and inscrutable. God never gets tired nor is He weak. He never grows weary, and He does not sleep. He is the *source* of strength that will never run dry. God and Jesus are the same.

God is the source of all we can see, and all we eat. He is the source of the air that we breathe. Everything begins with God. God and Jesus are the same.

His understanding is unsearchable and His knowledge is ungraspable. The Bible tells us in *Isaiah 55, His ways are higher than our ways and His thoughts are higher that our thoughts.* He is the source of all that there is. And God and Jesus are the same. Jesus is the visible image of God Himself.

▶ **God is Omnipotent**

Jeremiah 32:17, 27

'Ah Lord God! Behold, You have made the heavens and the earth by Your great power and outstretched arm. There is nothing too hard for You.

"Behold, I am the Lord, the God of all flesh. Is there anything too hard for Me?

Omnipotent means that God is All-Powerful. God's power is never ending. God's power is unsearchable. God's power is unparalleled. There is no one as powerful as God, or even remotely close to it. Jehovah is the very *essence* of power. God is the *source* of power and nothing or no one can ever overcome

God Almighty. He may think that he can, but his efforts will be utterly futile. Satan tried to overcome God and he is still paying the price for the intentions of his heart.

▶ **God is Omnipresent**

Psalms 139:7-10

Where can I go from Your Spirit? Or where can I flee from Your presence? If I ascend into heaven, You are there; if I make my bed in hell, behold, You are there. If I take the wings of the morning, and dwell in the uttermost parts of the sea, even there Your hand shall lead me, and Your right hand shall hold me.

Omnipresent means that God is everywhere at the same time. The earth is a fairly good-sized planet but it is one of the smallest planets in this solar system. The experts say that the earth is about 26,000 miles in circumference. That means there are approximately 676,000,000 square miles of earth. This is a lot of area. But God is everywhere at the same time. This is not to mention the eight other planets in our solar system and the millions of solar systems that our finite minds have knowledge of existence. God is just everywhere.

▶ **God is Omniscience**

1 John 3:20

For if our hearts condemns us, God is greater than our hearts, and knows all things.

Nothing takes God by surprise. I seriously doubt I took God by surprise in anything that I have ever done. I am pretty sure He didn't look down from heaven and say "Oh My Me! That's a shock. I would never have dreamed Michael would do that!" The Bible tells us He knows us from the end to the beginning. That is a comfort.

Our Relationship with God

To be *Christ-like* is to inherit the *attributes* of Christ by developing a relationship with God. Jesus set the *example* for us in our Christian walk, or the life of the Saint. Many times He separated himself from everyone, His disciples and even His family, to go into the hills to spend time with God. In *Luke 6:12*, we see the example He set for us:

"Now it came to pass in those days that He went out to the mountain to pray, and continued all night in prayer to God."

Through His actions, we may discover that a relationship with God is the most important part of being a Christian. Staying *connected* with the Father through His Spirit *enables* Him to call us sons and daughters of God. Having the attitude of prayer is the probably the most important thing that the Christian man and woman should exercise on a daily basis. A day without prayer is a day without power, a day without instruction, is a day without spiritual guidance. A day without prayer is a day wasted. *Romans 8:14* says:

For those who are led by the Spirit of God, these are sons of God."

The man or woman who claims to be a Christian or son/daughter of God should be in *contact* with God almost continuously. *Talking* to God and *listening* to His voice is essential in *developing* a relationship with Him. This is much like your relationship with your husband, wife, children, parents, or friends. You *know* their voice. You know their likes and dislikes, their personalities and so on. We need to know God in this way. Jesus, our true shepherd explains that when we have a relationship with Him we would know His voice.

194

John 10:1-5

"Most assuredly, I say to you, he who does not enter the sheepfold by the door, but climbs up some other way, the same is a thief and a robber. But he who enters by the door is the shepherd of the sheep. To him the doorkeeper opens, and the sheep hear his voice; and he calls his own sheep by name and leads them out. And when he brings out his own sheep, he goes before them; and the sheep follow him, for they know his voice. Yet they will by no means follow a stranger, but will flee from him, for they do not know the voice of a stranger."

Jesus is the only *door*, the only *way* into the Kingdom of God. He is the only truth that has the endorsement of God Almighty. Everyone before Him is false, and everyone that is not in Christ and preaches is also false. Today, we are to lead people to Christ and teach them in the ways of Christ. Anything outside that spectrum is false teaching.

There have been times in the life of the Christian when they are not sure if they are hearing from God or not. This may be due to the fact, the person who is new to the faith and the war that happens in the flesh is *vying* for the *dominant* position. The flesh does not like this new way of life because it has to *succumb* to the Spirit of God that dwells there. The flesh does not want to hear from God and the Spirit always wants to be in direct communion with God.

So how would one know if he/she is hearing from God or not? The first thing we must realize is *the voice must line up with His Word.* And it must be in the context in which it was spoken. There are some who will put Scriptures together that are totally out of line, such as; Judas went and hanged himself, go and do likewise. This sounds very far-fetched but a little leaven leavens the whole batch. A little *false statement* here and a little there and you will end up with a *false doctrine* which will be poisonous to whoever listens. Remember the *false religions* we read earlier in the book – these visiting angels who came to men were powerful and splendid but *their message did not line up* with the Word of God.

When we *hear* from God, we must be *obedient* to His *instructions*. If we are obedient to His instructions, we will be blessed. If we don't, we will miss out on God's blessing. People have paid a heavy penalty for not being obedient to the instructions of God while others have been blessed tremendously by God for their *obedience.*

The more you *hear* from God, the more *comfortable* you will be in hearing His voice. You will *recognize* His voice because you have spent time with the Father; you will be *accustomed* to His voice and the Word that He speaks. When the other voice comes, you will know it is false because the *peace of God* does not complement it. And when you do hear it, just say out loud – "That is not my Lord!"

Notes:

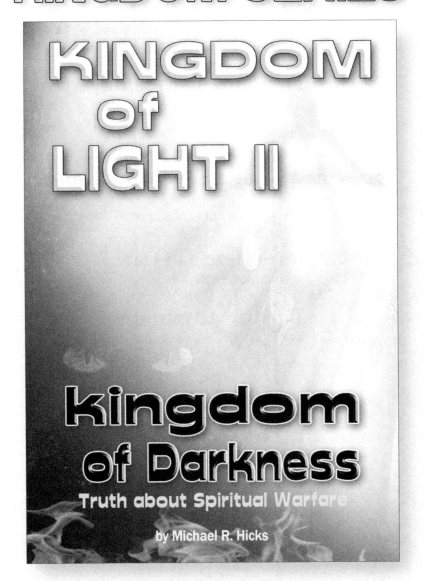

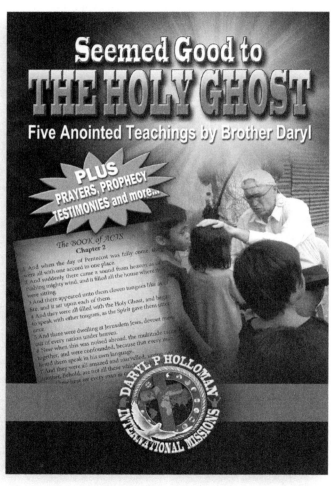

Printed in Great Britain
by Amazon

30668597R00126